REFLECTIONS
on the
GREAT TRUTHS
OF THE CHRISTIAN RELIGION
for
Every Day in the Month
BY
BISHOP
RICHARD CHALLONER

ISBN: 979-8-9911176-2-3

CONTENTS

3

Directions for the Use
of the following Considerations.

Make choice of a proper time and place for rec-
ollection; and shut the door of thy heart as much
as possible against the world, and its distracting
cares and affections.

2. Place thyself in the presence of God, representing him to thyself by a lively faith, as filling heav-
en and earth with his incomprehensible Majesty;
or as residing, with all his attributes, in the very
centre of thy own soul. Prostrate thyself in spirit
before him, to adore this sovereign Lord; make an
offering of thy whole self unto him, and humbly
beg pardon for all thy past treasons against him

3. Implore, with fervour and humility, his light
and grace, that the great truths of the Gospel may
make a due impression upon thy soul, that-thou
mayest effectually learn to fear him, and to love
him.

4. Read leisurely, and with serious attention, the
chapter for the day. Give the soul time to digest
what thou art reading; and pause more particularly on those points which affect thee most.

5. That thy reading may partake the more of the nature of mental prayer, strive to draw from thy considerations such affections as are suitable to the subject; by stirring up, for example, in, the soul, the fear and love of God, a confidence in his goodness, a sense of gratitude for his benefits, the horror of sin, and such like: open thy heart as much as thou canst to these affections, that so these great and necessary virtues may take the deeper root there.

6. Conclude thy considerations with holy resolutions of amendment of life, insisting in particular, on the failings to which thou art most subject, and firmly determining with thyself, to begin to put these resolutions into execution, on such occasions as may occur that very day,

7. Often reflect in the day time on the chief points of thy consideration; lest the enemy rob thy soul of this divine seed, by making thee quickly forget what thou hast been reading and considering.

THE FIRST DAY.

On the Necessity of Consideration

Consider, first, those words of the prophet Jeremias: "With desolation is the whole earth laid desolate, because there is no one who thinks in his heart." Jer. 12. v. 11. And reflect how true it is, that the want of consideration on the great truths of Christianity, is the chief source of all our evils. Alas! the greater part of men, seldom or never think either of their first beginning, or last end: they neither consider who brought them into the world, nor for what; nor reflect on the eternity into which they are just about to step. Hence all their pursuits are earthly and temporal, as if they were only made for this life, or were to be always here. Death, judgment, heaven, and hell, make but little impression upon them, because they don't give them time to sink deep into their souls by the means of serious Consideration. They run on, with their eyes shut, to the precipice of a miserable eternity, and only, then begin to think, when they find themselves lodged in that place of woe, where "their worm shall never die, and fire shall never be quenched." Ah! my poor soul, take care that this be not thy case.

2. Consider, that we cannot be saved without knowing God, and loving him above all things. Now, we can neither know him, nor love him as we ought, without the help of Consideration. It is this which discovers to us the infinite perfections of this sovereign Being, his heavenly beauty, his eternal love for us, and all the benefits which he has bestowed upon us, his most undeserving and ungrateful creatures: all which, alas! make no impression on us without serious consideration. All things that are about us, the heavens, the earth, and every creature therein, cease not to preach God unto us, and invite us to love him. But without Consideration, we are deaf to this voice of the whole creation; we are like those that have eyes and see not, that have ears and hear not. Ah! the great and dreadful mischiefs that follow from the want of the true knowledge of God, which is the fruit of frequent Consideration! Is it not upon this account that the whole world is overrun with wickedness; and that hell opens wide its jaws, devouring without end or number, the unhappy children of Adam, because God is forgotten, because there is no knowledge of God upon earth?" Osee, iv. 1,

3. Consider, that, to save our souls, we must also

know ourselves; we must know our misery and corruption, that we may be humble and diffident in ourselves; we must know our irregular inclinations and passions, that we may fight against them, and overcome them; we must study and watch the motions of our own hearts, that we may not be surprised by sin, and sleep in death. And how can this all-necessary knowledge of ourselves, this science of the saints, be acquired without the help of daily Consideration? Ah! how unhappy are they who know all things else, and are strangers to themselves! Let us then daily pray with St. Augustin, Noverim te, Noverim me; Lord, give me grace to know thee, Lord give me grace to know myself: and let us labour for these two most necessary sciences, by frequent consideration.

4. Consider, that in order to nourish in our souls the wholesome fear of God, which is the beginning of true wisdom, and spur ourselves on in the way of virtue, we must also seriously reflect on the enormity of sin, and the hatred God bears unto it; on the dreadful effect of sin in the soul, and on the multitude of our own sins in particular; on the vanity, misery and deceitfulness of the world; on the comfort and happiness that attend a virtuous life; on the shortness of time, and the dreadful

length of a miserable eternity; on the certainty and uncertainty of death, and the sentiments we shall have when we come to die; on the small number of the elect, &c. Ah! Christians, let us not neglect this great means of salvation! It was the consideration of these truths that made so many saints; that has so often reclaimed even the most abandoned sinners. Oh! what a profound lethargy must that soul be in, which is not roused at the thunder of those dreadful truths, death, judgment, hell, eternity!

5. Consider the bitter but fruitless repentance of the damned, condemning their past folly, in having thought so little on those things on which they shall now think for all eternity. Senseless wretches as we were! we had once our time, when, by thinking upon this miserable eternity, we might have escaped it. Those endless joys of heaven were offered us at a cheap rate, when a little reflection on them might have put us in the way of securing to ourselves the everlasting possession of them. But alas! we would not think then; and now it is too late. O my soul, learn thou to be wise by their misfortune; reflect in this thy day on the things that appertain to thy eternal peace; think well on thy last end; meditate on the great truths

of the gospel. Thou must either think of them now, or hereafter, when the thought of them will only serve to aggravate thy misery for all eternity.

THE SECOND DAY.

On the end of our creation.

CONSIDER, Christian soul, that so many years ago thou wast not yet come into the world, and that thy being was a mere nothing. The world had lasted near upon six thousand years, with innumerable transactions and revolutions in every nation; and where wast thou all that while? Alas! thou wast ingulphed in the deep abyss of nothing, infinitely beneath the condition of the meanest creature upon the earth; and what couldst thou do remaining there? Learn then to humble thyself, whatever advantages thou mayst enjoy of nature or grace, since of thyself thou art nothing; and all that thou hast above nothing has been given or lent thee by thy maker. Ah! poor wretch, what hast thou to be proud of? Or what canst thou call thy own, but nothing and sin, which is worse than nothing?

2. Consider, that the almighty hand of God, descending into that deep abyss of nothing, has drawn thee forth from thence, and given thee this being which thou now enjoyest, the most accomplished and perfect of any in this visible world, capable of knowing and loving God in this life, and designed for everlasting happiness with him in the next. Admire and adore the bounty of thy God, who from all eternity has designed this being for thee, preferably to so many millions of others which he has left behind, that had as fair a title to a being as thou hadst. Look forward into that immense eternity for which thou hast been created, and thankfully acknowledge, that the love thy God bears thee has neither beginning nor end, but reaches from eternity to eternity.

3. Consider, that being created by Almighty God, and having received thy whole being from him, by the justest of all titles thou belongest to him; and art obliged to consecrate to his service all thy powers, faculties and senses; and art guilty of a most crying injustice, as often as thou abusest any part of thy being, by employing it in the pursuit of vanity and sin. Ah! my poor soul, how little have we hitherto thought of this? How small a part of our thoughts, words and deeds, has been referred

to him who is our first beginning, and therefore ought to be the last end of all our actions? Be confounded at so great an abuse; repent and amend.

4. Consider, that God, who gave thee thy being, and who created all things else in this visible world for thy service, has created thee for himself alone. Not that he stood in need of thee, or can receive from thee any increase or addition to his happiness; but that he might give thee his grace in this life, and the endless joys of his kingdom in the next. Stand astonished, Christian soul, at the bounty of thy Creator, in making thee for so noble an end; and since thou wast made for God, be ashamed to content thyself with any thing less than God: learn then to contemn all that is earthly and temporal, as things beneath thee, and unworthy of thy affection. Lament thy past folly, and that of the far greater part of mankind, who spend their days in vain amusements, in restless cares about painted toys and mere trifles; and seldom or never think of that great end, for which alone they came into this world.

5. Consider that all the powers and faculties of thy soul, thy will, thy memory, thy understanding, and all the senses and parts of thy body, were

all given by thy Creator, as so many means to attain to this end of thy creation, to be employed during thy short abode in this transitory life, in the service of thy God, and so to bring thee to the eternal enjoyment of him in the sweet repose of his blessed kingdom. Alas! my soul, have we not perverted all these gifts of our maker, in turning them all against the giver? Have mercy on us, O Lord; have mercy on us; pardon our past treasons, and give us grace now to begin to be wise for eternity.

THE THIRD DAY.

On the benefits of God.

CONSIDER, my soul, how many and how great are thy obligations to the bounty of thy God. He has thought of thee from all eternity:

he has loved thee from all eternity: all the blessings and favours which he has bestowed upon thee in time, he designed for thee from all eternity; they are all the consequences of his eternal love for thee. Is it possible that so great a God, the most high and the most holy, who dwells in eternity, should set his affections upon such a poor sinful worm of the earth? Is it possible, my soul, that thou shouldst have had a place from all eternity in the heart of thy God; and that his eternal mind should never have been one moment without thinking on thee! Ah! poor wretch, what return hast thou made for this ancient love? How late hast thou loved him, who has loved thee from all eternity? How little hast thou thought of him, who always thinks of thee?

2. Consider that thy God has not only given thee by creation thy soul and body, with all their pow-

ers and faculties, and, in a word, whatever thou hast, and whatever thou art; but also preserves them each moment by the benefit of conservation, which may be called a continual creation. For as nothing but his Almighty hand could give thee this being, so none but he could preserve thee from falling back into thy former nothing: which must infallibly have happened to thee, if thy God had but for one moment withdrawn his supporting hand. Poor sinner! why didst thou not think of this when, by thy repeated crimes, thou wast waging war with thy God; and he with incomparable love was night and day watching over thee? How didst thou dare presume so often and for so long a time to provoke him, who held the thread of thy life in his hand, and who every moment could have crushed thee into nothing, or send thee headlong into hell! Oh! blessed by all creatures be his mercy for ever, for having borne with thee so long.

3. Consider the inestimable benefit of our redemption, by which our loving God has rescued us from sin, and from hell, the just reward of sin. Alas! my poor soul, we must have been lost for ever, had not this sovereign Maker and Lord of heaven and earth loved us to that degree, as to

deliver himself up to the most cruel and ignominious death of the cross for our redemption. Greater love than this no man hath, that one lay down his life for his friend: St. John xv. 13. But, O dear Lord, thou hast carried thy love much farther than this, in dying for those who by sin were thy declared enemies: in dying for such ungrateful wretches, as would scarce ever thank thee for thy love, and seldom or never so much as pity thy sufferings, or take any notice of them. Ah! Christians, what shall we most admire, to see this great monarch of heaven and earth, (in comparison with whom the whole creation is just nothing, or rather less than nothing,) expiring on a cross for such despicable worms as we are? Or to see those, who believe this amazing truth, take so little notice of this immense love, which will be a just subject of astonishment to men and angels for all eternity.

4. Consider how much we owe to God for having called us to the true faith, preferably to so many millions whom he has left behind in darkness and the shades of death. Alas! poor souls, how deplorable is their condition, void as they are of the knowledge of Jesus Christ, or of his only spouse, the true Catholic Church! How little do they

think of God, or of the life to come! With how little apprehension or remorse do they run on from sin to sin, and die impenitent! Ah! the goodness of God, that has not suffered us to fall into such misery, though born and bred up amidst a people seduced by error! Or, if we have also had the misfortune, like our neighbours, to have gone astray from the womb, has by a more distinguishing mercy drawn us out of the dragon's jaws, and brought us to his fold, the Catholic Church! Blessed be our God for ever for all his mercies. Oh! what an inestimable happiness it is, to have, by the means of this grace of vocation, God himself for our father, and his holy Church for our mother! Consider, first, those words of the prophet Jeremias : "With desolation is the whole earth laid desolate, because there is no one who thinks in his heart." Jer. 12. v. 11. And reflect how true it is, that the want of Consideration on the great truths of Christianity, is the chief source of all our evils. Alas! the greater part of men, seldom or never think either of their first beginning, or last end: they neither consider who brought them into the world, nor for what; nor reflect on the eternity into which they are just about to step. Hence all their pursuits are earthly and temporal, as if they were only made for this life, or were to be always here, Death, judgment, heaven, and hell, make but little impression upon them, because they don't give them time to sink deep into their souls by the means of serious Consideration. They run on, with their eyes shut, to the precipice of a miserable eternity, and only, then begin to think, when they find themselves lodged in that place of woe, where "their worm shall never die, and their

To pass this transitory life in the happy society of the only spouse of God's only son! To be daily partakers of the sacraments, those heavenly conduits of divine grace! To live and die in the communion of the saints, &:c. Ah! blessed is the people who have the Lord for their God: Ps. cxliii. 15.

5. Consider, Christian soul, whoever thou art, the particular providence of God towards thee! With how many graces he has presented thee from thy tender years: from how many misfortunes he has preserved thee! Has he not borne with thee for a long time, whilst others have been cut off in their sins? Are there not millions now burning in hell for less sins than thou hast committed? Reflect on the advantages thou hast received above thousands: what conveniencies of life, what friends, what health &c; whilst so many, more worthy

than thyself, have been abandoned to poverty and misery. Ah! admire the unspeakable goodness of thy God to thee: be astonished and confounded at thy past ingratitude: resolve from henceforth never to cease giving him thanks and blessing his name.

THE FOURTH DAY.

On the dignity and obligations of a Christian.

CONSIDER that every Christian by nature, and inasmuch as he is a man, is the most perfect of all visible creatures, endowed with understanding and reason; composed of a body whose structure is admirable, and of a spiritual and immortal soul, created to the image and likeness of God, and capable of the eternal enjoyment of him; enriched with a free will, and advanced by his Creator to the dignity of lord and master of all other creatures; though not designed to meet with his happiness in any of them, but in the Creator alone. Ah! my soul, hast thou hitherto been sensible of the dignity of thy nature? Hast thou not, too often, like brute beasts, looked no farther than this earth, that is, these present material and sensible things? Hast thou not too often made thyself a slave to creatures, which were only made to serve thee?

2. Consider that every Christian by grace, and inasmuch as he is a Christian, has been by the sacrament of baptism advanced to the participation of the divine nature, and made the adopted child

of God, heir of God, and co-heir with Christ. He has been made the temple of the Most High, consecrated by the sprinkling of the blood of Christ, and the unction of his grace; and has received at the same time an unquestionable right and title to an everlasting kingdom. O Christian soul, didst thou ever yet entertain a serious thought of the greatness of this dignity to which thou hast been raised at thy baptism? How has thy life corresponded with this dignity? O child of heaven, how long wilt thou be a slave to the earth?

3. Consider, that as the dignity of a Christian is very great, so also the obligations that attend this dignity are greater than the generality of Christians imagine. These obligations, in short, comprised in our baptismal engagement. The first condition upon which we were by baptism adopted into God's family, was that of faith. The minister of Christ examined us at the font upon every article of our belief; and to each interrogation we answered, by the mouths of our godfathers and godmothers, credo, I do believe. What has thy faith been, O my soul? Has it been conformable to this thy profession? Has it been firm without wavering? Has it been generous, so as not to be ashamed of the doctrine of thy heavenly Master,

or the maxims of his gospel? Has it shewed itself in thy actions? Or hast thou not been of the number of those whose life gives the lie to their faith? Of whom the apostle complains: Tit. i. 16. Who make profession of knowing God, but deny him by their works.

4. Consider, that at our baptism we made a solemn renunciation of the devil, and all his works, and all his pomps. Have we ever seriously reflected upon this renunciation? Or do we rightly understand the obligations of it? And yet our title to the inheritance of our heavenly Father is forfeited in the moment that we are false to this sacred engagement. Ah! my soul, if thou hast renounced satan, take care that in the practice of thy life, thou keep far from him: take care thou be no longer his slave by sin. Fly from all his works, the works of darkness: let him henceforth find nothing in thee that he may claim for his own, and by means of which he may also lay claim to thee. Despise his vain pomps, the false appearance of worldly grandeur, the prodigality, vanity, and sinful divertisements by which he allures poor worldlings into his nets: and if at any time thou art invited to take part in these fooleries, repeat to thyself those words of St. Augustine: "What hast

thou to do with the pomps of the devil, which thou hast renounced?"

5. Consider, that at baptism each one of us, according to the ancient ceremony of the Catholic Church, was clothed with a white garment, which the minister of Christ gave us with these words: receive this white garment, which thou shalt carry without spot or stain before the judgment-seat of Christ. Happy souls, that comply with this obligation! What a comfort will it be to them in life, what a joy and satisfaction in death, to have kept this robe of innocence undefiled! But, O baptismal innocence, where shall we find thee in this unhappy age? O blindness and stupidity of the children of Adam, that part so easily with such an inestimable treasure! Alas! my poor soul, has it not been thy misfortune? Oh! make haste to wash away, with penitential tears, those dreadful stains of sin, which otherwise must be the eternal fuel of hell's merciless flames.

THE FIFTH DAY.

On the Vanity of the world.

CONSIDER these words of the wisest of men: Eccles. i. 2. Vanity of vanities, and all is vanity: and reflect how truly vain are all those things which deluded worldlings seek with so much eagerness; honours, riches and worldly pleasures are all but painted bubbles, which look at a distance as if they were something, but have nothing of real substance in them; and, instead of a solid content and joy, bring nothing with them but a trifling satisfaction for a moment, followed with cares, uneasiness, apprehensions and remorse. Ah! bubbles indeed, which their admirers no sooner offer to lay hold of, but they dissolve into air, and leave their hands empty! Oh! how justly were all worldly enjoyments by the royal prophet likened to a dream! They have slept out their short sleep, and when they awake they find nothing in their hands of all those things which, in their dream, they seemed to possess. O ye sons of men, how long will ye be in love with vanity, and run after lies? Psalm iv. 3.

2. Consider that saying of St. Augustine, L. i. Con-

fes. C. 1. Thou hast made us, O Lord, for thyself; and our hearts cannot rest till they rest in thee: and reflect, that our great Creator has given us a noble soul, made to his own image, and like him spiritual and immortal; which therefore can never find its happiness in earthly and fading things. No, my soul, thou hast an understanding and a will capable of contemplating the sovereign beauty and sovereign truth, and of enjoying the one supreme infinite good; and whatever is less than He, is not worthy of thee. Ah! resolve then no longer to tire thyself, and waste away thy spirits in running like a child after these butterflies; but since thou canst not be without seeking for happiness, seek it in God's name, where it is to be found, that is, in the way of virtue and devotion; and not in the by-paths which lead to endless misery.

3. Consider the shortness of all worldly enjoyments. Man's days are very short: the longest life is less than one moment, if compared with eternity. A thousand years, in the sight of God, that is, in very truth, are but as yesterday that is past and gone: Psalm lxxxix. 4. Alas! does not daily experience shew us, that we are here to-day, and gone to-morrow, and no sooner out of sight, but out

of mind too? For as soon as we are in the grave, those that we leave behind think no more of us. All flesh is grass, says the Prophet Isaiah, chap. xl. 6. and all the glory of it but like that of the flower of the field. And what is that, but flourishing in the morning, and fading in the evening? Oh! how truly is our life likened by St. James, chap. iv. to a vapour; a thin smoke, which is dispersed by the first puff of wind, and we see no more of it? How justly is it compared by Solomon, Wisdom, chap. v. to a shadow, or to the passing of a bird upon the wing, or an arrow from the bow, which leaves no mark behind it? Ah! how vain it is to set our hearts upon what we must leave so soon!

4. Consider, what is now become of all those great ones of this world, those mighty monarchs, those gallant generals, those wise statesmen, those cel-ebrated beauties &c; who made such a figure a hundred years ago? Alas! they are all long since dead and gone; and now few or none ever think of them, or scarce know there ever were any such persons; just so will it be with us a few years hence. Ah! worldlings, give ear for one moment to those who are gone before you, who, from their silent monuments, where the remainder of their dust lies mingled with the common earth, call

upon you in the words of the wise man: Eccles. xxxviii. 23. Remember what we are come to; it will soon be the same with you; it was our turn yesterday; it will be yours to-day. We once had our parts to act upon the stage of the world; we once were young, strong, and healthy, as you are now, and thought as little as you of what we are now come to: like you, we set our hearts upon those trifles and toys, that we could but enjoy for a moment; and for these we neglected eternity. Senseless wretches as we were! we chose rather to be slaves to a cheating world, to inconstant, perishable creatures, which abandoned us so soon, than to serve that Lord and Master to whom nothing dies; and who neither in life nor death ever forsakes those who forsake not him. Christians, let us take this warning; let the miscarriages of so many others teach us to be wise; let us not set our hearts on this miserable world; nor look upon any thing as truly great, but that which is eternal.

THE SIXTH DAY.

On the happiness of serving God.

CONSIDER these words of the Prophet Isaiah: say to the just man, it is well: Isai. iii. 10. and reflect on the manifold advantages which this short world well comprises and ensures to the just, both for time and eternity. Honour, riches and pleasure, are the things on which the world sets the greatest value. But they are not to be found where the world seeks them, but only in the service of God. Can any honour upon earth be compared to that of being a servant, a friend, an adopted son of the great king of heaven? Such a soul is far more dignified, in the eyes of God and his angels than the greatest emperor in the universe. She is a child of the eternal Father, a spouse of the eternal son, a temple of the eternal spirit; heiress of the kingdom of heaven, and sister and companion to the angels. Oh! my soul, let such honours as these be the only object of thy ambition.

2. Consider that the truest riches are to be found in the service of God; not, indeed, always those worldly possessions, which are attended with so many cares and fears; which are daily exposed to

so many accidents, and which are not capable of satisfying the heart: but the inestimable treasure of the grace of God, which is the seed of everlasting glory; the gifts of the Holy Ghost; the love of God; in a word, God himself; whom the whole world cannot take from the soul, unless she be so miserably blind as to drive him away by mortal sin. Add to this the fatherly providence of God over the just; that his eyes are always upon them to take care of their welfare; that his angels always encamp about them to guard them by night and by day: Ps. xxxiii. v. 8. that, as he formerly said to Abraham, Gen. xv. he himself is their protector, and their reward exceeding great. He is their friend, and the best of friends; the shepherd of their souls, who leads them out to his admirable pastures, to the fountains of living water. His tenderness towards them is beyond that of a father, nay, beyond that of the tenderest mother: Isaiah xlix. 15, 16. In short, God is all things to those that fear him. Oh! my soul, seek no other treasure than him. Fear nothing but the losing of him If thou hast him, nothing can make thee miserable; but without him, nothing can make thee happy.

3. Consider the pleasure that attends a virtuous life; the satisfaction, peace and joy of a good con-

science, which, by the wise man, is likened to a continual banquet; the consolations of the Holy Ghost; the comfortable expectation of a happy eternity after our exit out of this vale of tears; a holy confidence in the protection and providence of God, and a perfect conformity in all things to his blessed will. From these fountains flow such delights, as cannot be conceived by worldlings who have no experience of them: pleasures pure and spiritual, which sweeten all the crosses of this life, are an unspeakable comfort in death, and carry with them a certain foretaste of the immortal joys of heaven. Whereas all worldly pleasures, like the world itself, are false and deceitful; always be-sprinkled with something of bitterness, and attended with uneasiness, followed by remorse, and end at last in eternal sorrow.

4. Consider that saying of our Saviour, one thing is necessary: Luke x. 42. And what is that one thing, O my soul, which alone can make thee happy, both here and hereafter? It is to serve thy God, and to provide in earnest for eternity. All time compared to eternity is less than nothing. So are all temporal concerns, if compared with the concerns of eternity. This, in reality, is thy only business; if thou take care of this, all is well; if thou

neglect this, all is lost, and lost for ever. As for all other things of which thou sayest stand in need in this life, give ear again to the same Saviour: Mat. vi. 33. Seek first the kingdom of God and his justice, and all these things shall be given you over and above. Conclude then, my soul, since both thy temporal and eternal welfare depends on serving God, to make this for the future thy only care. Thus only shalt thou meet true comfort here: thus only shalt thou come to never-ending happiness hereafter.

THE SEVENTH DAY.

On death.

CONSIDER, that there is nothing more certain than death. It is appointed for all men once to die; and, after that, judgment. The sentence is general; it is pronounced upon all the children of Adam: neither wealth, nor strength, nor wisdom, nor all the power of this world can exempt any one from this common doom. From the first moment of our birth, we are hastening to our death: every moment brings it nigher to us. The day will come, it will certainly come, and only God knows how soon, when we shall never see the night: or the night will come, when we shall never see the ensuing morning. The day will most certainly come, when thou, my soul, must bid a long farewell to this cheating world, and all thou hast admired therein; and even to thy own body, the individual companion of thy life; and take thy journey to another country, where all that thou settest a value upon here, will appear as smoke: learn then to despise this miserable world, and all its enjoyments, with which thou must part so soon, whether thou wilt or not.

2. Consider, that as nothing is more certain and inevitable than death, so nothing is more uncertain than the time, the place, the manner, and all other circumstances of our death. "O my soul," says St. Francis Sales, "thou must one day part with this body: but when shall that day be? Shall it be in winter or in summer? In the city or in the country? By day or by night? Shall it be suddenly, or on notice given thee? Shalt thou have leisure to make thy confession? Shalt thou have the assistance of thy ghostly father? Alas! of all this thou knowest nothing at all: only certain it is, that thou must die; and that, as it almost always happens, much sooner than thou imaginest."

3. Consider, that death being so certain, and the time and manner of it so uncertain, it would be no small comfort, if a man could die more than once, that so, if he should have the misfortune once to die ill, he might repair the fault by taking more care a second time. But, alas! we can die but once; and when once we have set our foot within the gates of eternity, there is no coming back. If we die once well, it will be always well: but if once ill, it will be ill for all eternity. Oh! dreadful moment, upon which depends an endless eternity! O blessed Lord, prepare us for that fatal hour!

4. Consider the folly and stupidity of the greater part of men, who, though they daily see some or other of their friends, acquaintance, or neighbours carried off by death, and that very often in the vigour of their youth, very often by sudden death, yet always imagine death to be at a distance from them: as if those arrows of death, which are falling on all sides of them, would not reach them too in their turn; or as if they had a greater security than so many others who are daily swept away. Senseless worldlings! Why will you not open your eyes? Why would you fondly imagine yourselves secure from the stroke of death, when you cannot so much as promise yourselves one single day of life? How many will die before the end of this month, that are as young, as strong, and as healthy as you are? Who knows but you may be of that number? Ah! Christians, take care lest you be surprised. Set your house in order: and for the future fly from sin, the only evil which makes death terrible. Live always in those dispositions in which you would gladly be found at the hour of your death. To act otherwise, is to renounce both religion and reason.

5. Consider the state and condition of this corruptible body of ours, as soon as we are dead.

Alas! it immediately becomes pale, stiff, loathsome, and hideous; insomuch, that our dearest
friends can scarce endure to watch one night in
the same room with it, much less bear to lie in the
same bed. And so fast does it tend to stench and
corruption, that its nearest relations are the first to
desire to get it out of the house, and to lay it deep
under ground, that it may not infect the air. But
what companions, what attendants, must it meet
with there? Worms and maggots. For these, O
man, thou art pampering thy body: these are to be
thy inheritance, or rather, they are to inherit thee:
whatever thou art to-day, to-morrow thou art to
be the food of worms. Ah! worldlings, that are
enamoured with your own and others' beauty, and
thereby too often drawn from your allegiance to
God, vouchsafe for once to reflect upon the condition to which both you and they must so soon
be reduced, and you will see what little reason
you have to set your affections upon these painted
dunghills, which will so quickly betray what they
are, and end in noisomeness and corruption. We
read that St. Francis Borgia was so touched with
the bare sight of the ghastly countenance of the
empress Isabella after death, whom he had seen a
little before in all her majesty, and all her charms,
as to conceive an eternal disgust of this world, and

a happy resolution of consecrating himself wholly to the service of that king who never dies. Let the like consideration move us to the like resolution.

THE EIGHTH DAY.

On the sentiments we shall have
at the hour of our death.

CONSIDER, Christian soul, what will be thy sentiments at the hour of death with regard to this world, and all its perishable goods, vain honours, false riches and cheating pleasures. Alas! the world must then end in thy regard; it will turn upside down before thy eyes; and thou wilt begin to see clearly the nothingness of all those things on which thou hast here set thy heart. How wilt thou then despise all worldly honours and preferments, when thou seest thyself at the brink of the grave, where the worms will make no distinction between the king and the beggar! How little account wilt thou then make of the esteem of men, who now will think no more of thee? How wilt thou undervalue thy riches, which must now be left behind thee, when six foot of land, a coffin and a shroud, will be all thy possession? How despicable will all worldly pleasures then seem to thee, which, at the best, could never give thee any true satisfaction, and now fly from thee, and dissolve into smoke in thy sight! Ah! my poor soul, enter now into the same sentiments which thou shalt certainly have at the hour of thy death: thus, and only thus, thou shalt be out of danger of being deceived by this deceitful world.

2. Consider, what will then be thy thoughts with regard to thy sins; when the curtain will begin to be withdrawn, with which thy busy self-love has industriously hidden or disguised the deformity and malice of thy crimes: and they shall be set before thy eyes in their true light: when so many things which thou wast willing to persuade thyself were but small faults, or none at all, will present themselves before thee in other kind of colours, as great and hideous offences: when that false conscience, which thou hast framed to thyself, and under the cover of which thou hast passed over many things in thy confessions, as light and inconsiderable, which thou wast ashamed to declare, or unwilling to forsake, shall no longer be able to maintain itself at the approach of death. Ah! what anguish, what confusion, what dreadful temptations of despair must such a sight as this give to the dying sinner? Learn thou, my soul, to take better measures now in time, and thus to prevent so great a misery.

3. Consider, and take a nigher view of the lam-

entable state of a sinner at the hour of his death: when all things seem to conspire against him, and whichever way he looks for any ease or comfort, he can find none. Before his eyes he sees a whole army of sins mustered up; a viper's brood of his own offspring, which stick close to him, and, assailing him with their united forces, make him already begin to feel the gripes of that never-dying worm of conscience, which shall be the eternal torment of the damned. Oh! how gladly would he shake off this troublesome company: but all in vain; they are resolved not to leave him. If he looks back into his past life, to seek for some good works, to oppose to this army of sins; alas! he finds the good that he has done has been so inconsiderable, so insignificant, as to give him no hopes of its weighing down the scales, when balanced with his multiplied crimes. His very prayers, the confessions and communions which he has made, fly now in his face, and upbraid him with his wretched negligence, and his sacrilegious abuse of these great means of salvation. The sight of all things about him, his wife, his children, his friends, his worldly goods, which he has loved more than his God, serve for nothing now but to increase his anguish. And what is his greatest misery is, that the agonies of his sickness give him little or no leisure or ability to apply himself seriously to the greatest and most difficult of all concerns, which is, a perfect conversion to God after a long habit of sin. Oh! how truly may the sinner now repeat those words of the Psalmist: the sorrows of death have encompassed me, and the perils of hell have found me: Psalm cxiv. 3. Oh! what unspeakable anguish must it be to see himself just embarking upon eternity, an infinite and endless duration, an immense ocean, to whose further shore the poor sailor can never reach; and to have so much reason to fear, it will be to him an eternity of woe.

4. Consider, my soul, what thy sentiments will be at the hour of thy death, with relation to the service of God, to virtue and devotion: how lovely then will the way of virtue appear to thee! How wilt thou then wish to have followed that charming path! Oh! what a satisfaction is it to a dying man to have lived well! What a comfort to see himself now at the end of all his labours and dangers; to find himself at the gates of eternal rest, of everlasting peace, after a long and doubtful war! He may now securely come down from his watchtower, and repose himself for ever in the kingdom of his father. Oh! what a pleasure, what

a joy to look forward into that blessed eternity! Oh! how precious in the sight of God is the death of his saints: Psalm cxv. 15. Ah! Let my soul die the death of the just, and let my last end be like to theirs: Numb. xxiii. Christians, if we would die the death of the just, we must live the life of the just! The only security for a good death, is a good life.

5. Consider, or rather conclude, from the foregoing considerations on death, to make it the whole business of your life to prepare for death. Upon dying well depends nothing less than eternity. If we die ill, we are lost, and lost for ever. As then we came into the world for nothing else but to provide for eternity, so we may truly say, we came into the world for nothing else but to learn to die well. This is the great lesson we must all study. Alas! if we miss it, when we are called to the trial, an endless woe must of necessity be the consequence. Ah! how hard it is to learn to perform that well which can be done but once.

THE NINTH DAY.

On the particular judgment after death.

CONSIDER, that the soul is no sooner parted from the body, but she is immediately presented before the Judge, in order to give an account of her whole life, of all that she has thought, said or done, during her abode in the body; and to receive sentence accordingly. For that the eternal doom of every soul is decided by a particular judgment immediately after death, is what we learn from the gospel in the example of Dives and Lazarus: and the sentence that passes here will be ratified in the general judgment at the last day. Christians, how stand your accounts with God? What could you be able to say for yourselves if this night you should be cited to the bar? It may perhaps be your case. Remember that your Lord will come when you least expect him; take care then to be always ready.

2. Consider how exact, how rigorous his judgment will be, where even the least idle word cannot escape the scrutiny of the Judge. Oh! what treasures of iniquity will here come to light, when the veil shall be removed, which hides at present

the greatest part of our sins from the eyes of the world, and even from our own; and the whole history of our lives shall at once be exposed to our view. Good God! who can be able to bear this dreadful sight? Here shall the poor soul be brought to a most exact examination of all that she has done, or left undone, in the whole time of her pilgrimage in this mortal body: how she has corresponded with the divine inspirations; what use she has made of God's graces; what profit she has reaped from the sacraments which she has received; from the word of God which she has heard or read; what advantage she has made of those favourable circumstances in which God Almighty has placed her; how she has employed the talents with which he has entrusted her: even her best works shall be nicely sifted; her prayers, her fasts, her almsdeeds; the intention with which she has undertaken them; the manner in which she has performed them: all shall be weighed, not in the deceitful balance of the judgment of men , but in the scales of the sanctuary. Ah! how many of our actions will here be found to want weight, according to that of Dan. v: Thou hast been weighed in the balance, and art found of too little weight. Oh I enter not into judgment with thy servant, O Lord; for no man living shall be justified in thy sight. Ps. cxlii.

3. Consider the qualities of the Judge before whom we must appear. He is infinitely wise, and therefore cannot be deceived; he is infinitely powerful, and therefore cannot be withstood; lie is infinitely just, and therefore will render to every one according to his works. No favour is to be expected at this day: the time of merit and of acceptable repentance is now at an end. Ah! Christians, think well on it now whilst it is your day: you may now wash away your sins by penitential tears, and thus hide them from the eyes of your future Judge: you may at present tie up his hands by humble prayer; you may appeal from his justice to the court of his mercy, and cause him to cancel the sentence that stands against you: but at that day you will find him inexorable: your prayers and tears will then come too late.

4. Consider the inestimable comfort that the souls of the just shall receive at this day from the company of their good works, which, like an invincible rampart, shall surround them on all sides, and keep their hellish foes at a distance. Oh! my soul, let us take care to provide ourselves with such attendants as these against that hour, which

is to decide our eternal doom. These are friends indeed, that will not forsake us even in death; and will effectually plead our cause at that bar where no other eloquence will be regarded.

5. Consider in what a wretched plight the sinner, who has taken no care to lay up any such provision of good works, shall now stand before his Judge. Oh! how all things now speak to him the melancholy sentence, that is just now going to fall upon his guilty head. Whatever way he looks, he sees nothing that can give him any comfort; but, on the contrary, all things contribute to his greater anguish and terror. Beneath his feet he sees hell open ready to swallow him up: above his head, an angry Judge prepared to thunder out against him the irrevocable sentence of eternal damnation: on his right hand, he sees his guardian angel now abandoning him; on his left, the devils, his merciless enemies, just ready to seize upon him, and only waiting for the beck of the Judge: if he looks behind him, he discovers a cheating world which now retires from him; if he looks before him, he meets with nothing but a dismal eternity. Within him he feels the intolerable stings of a guilty conscience: and on all sides of him he perceives an army of hideous monsters, his own sins, more

terrible to him now than the furies of hell. Good God! deliver me from ever having any share in such a scene of misery.

6. Consider, that in order to prevent the judgment of God from falling heavy upon us after our death, we must take care, now during our life, to judge and chastise ourselves, by doing serious penance for our sins. Thus, and only thus, shall we disarm the justice of God enkindled by our sins. Let us follow the advice of him who is to be our Judge, who calls upon us to watch and pray at all times, that so we may be found worthy to escape these dreadful dangers, and stand with confidence before the Son of man: Luke xxi. 36. Ah! let this judgment be always before our eyes: let us daily meditate on this account that we are one day to give. Let us never forget that there is an eye above that sees all things; that there is an ear that hears all things; that there is a hand that writes down all our thoughts, words and deeds, in the great accounting book; and that all our actions pass from our hands to the hands of God; and what is done in time, passeth not away with time, but shall subsist after all time is past. Oh! that men would be wise, and would understand these truths, and provide in earnest for their last end! Deuter. xxxii.

THE TENTH DAY.

On the great accounting day.

CONSIDER, that nothing can be conceived more terrible than the prospect which scripture gives us of the last accounting day, with all the prodigies that shall go before it. The sun shall be darkened; the moon red as blood; the stars without light, and seeming to fall from the firmament; the earth shaken with violent earthquakes; the sea swelling and roaring with unusual tempests; the elements all in confusion, and whole nature in disorder. The day of the Lord, says the prophet Joel, ii. a day of darkness and obscurity, a day of clouds and whirlwinds. Before its face devouring fire, and behind it burning flames. The earth shall tremble at the appearance of it, and the heavens be moved at its sight. The sun and moon are darkened, and the stars have withdrawn all their light. And the prophet Sophonias, i. cries out: That day, a day of wrath, a day of tribulation and anguish, a day of calamity and misery, a day of darkness and obscurity, a day of mists and whirlwinds. Can any thing be more frightful than these descriptions? Ah! what will then be the thoughts of sinful man, who sees himself threatened by all these signs? Alas!

he shall perfectly wither away with fear, in expectation of that tragedy which must follow these dreadful preludes.

2. Consider, that the last day being come, a fire raging like an impetuous torrent shall, by the command of God, consume the whole surface of the earth, and all that is thereon; nothing shall escape it. Where, O worldlings, will be then all your stately palaces, your pleasant seats, your gardens, fountains and grottos? Where your gold, silver and precious stones &c.? Alas! all that you have set your hearts on in this world, shall in a moment be reduced into ashes; to shew you the vanity of the things you loved, and your own folly in placing your affection upon such glittering shadows, upon such painted bubbles. Learn then, my soul, to despise this world and all its goods, since all must end in ashes and smoke; and lay up for thyself a treasure in heaven, which alone will be out of the reach of this last fire.

3. Consider, that the final end of this world being now come, the archangel shall sound the last trumpet, and raise his voice with a Surgite mortui: Arise, ye dead, and come to judgment: a voice, that shall be heard at once all over the uni-

verse, that shall pierce the highest heavens, and penetrate down to the lowest abyss of hell: at this voice, in an instant, by God's almighty power, all the children of Adam, from the first to the last, shall arise from the dust, and every soul shall be again united to its respective body, never more to part for eternity. Oh! my soul, let this last trumpet always echo in thy ears! Oh! take care to prevent the terror of this summons, by hearkening now to another summons of the great trumpet of the Holy Ghost, who calls upon thee by the mouth of the apostle: Arise thou that sleepest, and rise from the dead, that is from the death of sin, and Christ shall enlighten thee, Eph. v. It is thus by having part in the first resurrection, thou shalt provide in time against that dreadful hour, when time shall be no more, Apoc. x. It is thus thou shalt escape the second death.

4. Consider the wonderful difference there will be at the time of this general resurrection between the bodies of the just and those of the wicked. The just shall arise in bodies most beautiful, more pure than the stars, more resplendent than the sun, immortal and impassible: but the wicked shall arise in bodies suitable to their deserts; foul, black, hideous, and every way loathsome and in-

supportable; immortal, it is true, but to no other
end than to endure immortal torments. What
an inexpressible rack will it be to these wretched
souls, to be forced into such carcasses, to be condemned to an eternal confinement in so horrid,
so filthy an abode! Ah! take thou care, my soul, to
keep thy body now pure from the corruption of
carnal sins, lest otherwise it be one day an aggravation of thy eternal misery.

5. Consider, with how much satisfaction and
joy the souls of the just shall be united again to
their bodies, which they have so long desired;
with what affection they shall embrace those fel-
low-partners of all their labours, of all their sufferings and mortifications; and now designed,
by sharing in the glory of the heavenly Sion, to
give an addition to their eternal happiness. But,
Oh! what dreadful curses shall pass at the melancholy meeting of the souls and bodies of the
reprobate! Accursed carcass! will the soul say, was
it to please thee, to indulge thy brutish inclinations, that I have forfeited the immortal joys of
heaven? Ah! wretch, to give thee a filthy pleasure
for a moment, I have damned both myself and
thee to all eternity. O thrice accursed carrion! it is
just, it is just, that thou who hast been the cause

of my damnation, shouldst be my partner in eternal woe. But oughtest not thou rather, unhappy soul, to be a thousand times accursed by the body, since it was thy business, and was in thy power, to have subjected its passions and lusts to the rule of reason and religion; and thou didst rather choose, for the sake of a momentary satisfaction, to enslave thyself to its sensual inclinations, and so to purchase hell both for thyself and thy body? Ah! Christians, let us learn to be wise by the consideration of others' misfortunes.

THE ELEVENTH DAY.

On the general judgment.

CONSIDER, that the dead being all risen shall immediately be assembled together in the place designed for the last judgment, commonly believed to be the valley of Josaphat, near Jerusalem, in the sight of mount Olivet and mount Calvary, where our Lord heretofore shed his blood for our redemption. What a sight will it be to behold here all the children of Adam, that innumerable multitude of all nations, ages and degrees, standing together without any distinction now of rich or poor, great or little, master or servant, monarch or subject; excepting only the distinction of good and bad, which shall be wonderful and eternal. Alas! how mean a figure will an Alexander or a Caesar make at this appearance, or any of those great heroes of antiquity, whose very name has made whole nations tremble? Those mighty monarchs, who had once the world at their beck, are now levelled with the meanest of their slaves, and would wish a thousand times never to have borne the sceptre, nor worn the diadem.

2. Consider, that the dead being now assembled

altogether, the great Judge shall descend from heaven, with great glory and majesty, environed with all his heavenly courtiers and all the legions of angels. Oh! how different from his first coming will this second appearance be! His first coming was in great meekness and humility, because that was our day, in which he came to redeem us by his mercy: but at his second coming, it will be his day, when he shall arm himself with all the terrors of his justice, to revenge upon sinful man the cause of his injured mercy, with a final vengeance once for all. Miserable sinners! how will you be able to stand before his face, or endure his wrathful countenance? Ah! then it is you will begin to cry out to the mountains and rocks to fall upon you, and hide you from the face of him that sitteth on the throne, and from the wrath of the Lamb. Nay, such a dread and terror will the very sight of the incensed Judge carry with it, that you will even wish a thousand times to hide your guilty heads in the lowest hell, rather than endure this dreadful appearance: but all in vain; you must stand it out

3. Consider, that, before the Judge, shall be borne the royal standard of the cross shining more bright than the sun, to the great comfort of the

good, and the unspeakable anguish and confusion of the wicked, for having made so little use of the inestimable benefit of their redemption. Here they shall plainly see how much their God has suffered for their salvation: how great has been his love for them, that boundless and unparalleled love, which brought him down from the throne of glory, and nailed him to the cross. Oh! how will they now condemn their own obstinacy in sin, their blindness and ingratitude! Oh! how will this glorious ensign justify, in the face of the whole universe, the conduct of God and the eternity of hell's torments: for what less than a miserable eternity can be punishment enough for so much obstinacy in evil, after so much love?

4. Consider, how at the command of the Sovereign Judge, which shall be instantly obeyed, the servants of God shall be picked out from the midst of that vast multitude, and placed with honour on his right hand; whilst the wicked, with all those evil spirits whose part they have taken, shall with ignominy be driven to the left. Oh! dreadful and eternal separation, after which these two companies shall never more meet. And thou, my soul, where dost thou expect to stand at that day? In which of these two companies shalt thou be

ranked? Thou hast it now in thy choice: choose then now that better part, which will never be taken from thee. Fly now from the midst of Babylon; renounce now the false maxims, the corrupt customs, and sinful divertisements of worldlings; separate thyself from the wicked in time, that thou mayest not be involved in their eternal damnation.

5. Consider, what then will be the thoughts of the great ones of this world; what fury, what envy, what bitter anguish and confusion will oppress their souls; when they shall see the poor in spirit, the meek and humble, who were so contemptible in their eyes, whilst they were here in this mortal life, now honoured and exalted in the sight of the whole universe; and themselves treated with so much contempt? Hearken to their complaints, as they are set down by the wise man: Wisd. v. These are they, whom heretofore we laughed at, and whom we made the subjects of our scoffs. Senseless wretches as we were! We esteemed their life madness, and their end without honour. See how they are now reckoned amongst the children of God, and with the saints is their eternal lot. Therefore we have erred from the way of truth. Alas! after all, we are the persons that have been

mistaken; we, that have unfortunately run on in the wrong way! And they were truly wise in making a better choice, which afforded them comfort in life, and has now entitled them to endless joys.

6. Consider, how much the anguish and confusion of the wicked will be increased, at the opening of the books of conscience, when all the guilt of their whole lives shall be laid open to the public view of the universe. Poor sinner! what will thy thoughts be, when those crimes, which thou hast committed in the greatest secrecy, and which thou wouldst not have known for the world; those abominations, which thou imaginedst covered with the obscurity of night and darkness, and which thou didst flatter thyself thy friends and acquaintance would never know; those works of iniquity which perhaps thou couldst not find in thy heart to discover to one person, tied by all laws to a perpetual secresy, shall all now be exposed in their true colours, to the eyes of the whole world, angels and men, good and bad, to thy eternal shame. Ah! Christians, it is now in your power to prevent, by a sincere repentance and confession, this confusion which you must otherwise one day suffer.

THE TWELFTH DAY.

On the last sentence of the good and bad.

CONSIDER, how this great trial shall be concluded by a final definitive sentence in favour of the just, and for the condemnation of the wicked. And first, the Sovereign Judge, turning himself towards his elect, with a most sweet and amiable countenance, shall invite them into the happy mansions of everlasting bliss: Come ye blessed of my Father, take possession of the kingdom prepared for you from the beginning of the world: Mat. xxv. O happy invitation! Happy, thrice happy they, that shall be found worthy to hear that comfortable sentence! What unspeakable satisfaction, what torrents of joy and pleasure will the hearing of it give to those blessed creatures! I am filled with joy, says the royal prophet, at the happy tidings which I have heard; we are to enter into the house of the Lord: Ps. cxxi. But, Oh! what envy, what rage and malice will the reprobate feel at the hearing of this invitation, when they shall see several of their acquaintance called to take possession of that eternal kingdom, which they might also have so easily purchased; but by their own folly and stupidity, have blindly exchanged it for the flames of hell.

2. Consider, and ponder at leisure upon this happy sentence: Come, says the Judge, ye blessed of my Father, &c. Come from the vale of tears where, for a little while, you have been tried and afflicted by the appointment of my providence, to the kingdom of never-ending joys; where grief and sorrow will be no more. Come from the place of banishment, where for a time you have sighed and groaned at a distance from your heavenly country, to your everlasting home, where you shall meet with all that your heart can desire to complete your happiness; where you shall be for ever inebriated by the plenty of my house, and drink for ever at the fountain of life: arise, my beloved, the winter is now past, the floods and storms are over, arise and come. O universal and eternal blessings! How my poor soul contemns all other happiness, in hopes of having a share one day in this blessed sentence!

3. Consider, how the great Judge, after having invited the just to his glorious kingdom, turning himself towards the wicked on his left hand, with fire in his eyes and terror in his countenance, shall thunder out against them the dreadful sentence of

their eternal doom in these words: go from me ye cursed into everlasting fire, which was prepared for the devil and his angels. Christian souls, weigh well every word of this dismal sentence. Go for ever from me, and from the joys of my kingdom. O terrible excommunication! O cruel divorce! O eternal banishment! Who can express, who can conceive what it is to be for ever separated from our God, our first beginning and last end, our great and sovereign good! Ah! wretches, who make so little now of losing your God by mortal sin, what will you then think when you shall be sentenced to this eternal banishment from him, doomed to seek him for all eternity, and yet, never to meet with him in any of his attributes, only in his avenging justice, the weight of which you shall feel for ever. But take notice whither you are to go, when you go from your God. Alas! into everlast-ing fire, there to lead an ever-dying life, there to endure a never-ending death, in the company of the devil and his angels; to whom you made your-selves slaves, and who shall now, without control, exercise forever their tyranny over you.

4. Consider that dreadful and universal curse which this just but dismal sentence involves. Go from me, ye cursed, says the Sovereign Judge: as

if he was to say: go, depart from me, but let my curse go with you. I would have given you my blessing, but you would not have it; a curse you chose, and a curse shall be your everlasting inheritance. It shall stick close to you like a garment for all eternity; it shall enter into your very bowels, and search into the very marrow of your bones. A curse upon your eyes, never to see the least glimpse of comfortable light: a curse upon your ears, to be entertained for all eternity with frightful shrieks and groans: a curse on your taste, to be for ever imbittered with the gall of dragons: a curse on your smell, to be always tormented with the noisome stench of the pit of hell: a curse on your feeling and on all the members of your body, to burn and never consume in that fire which shall never be quenched: a curse upon your understanding, never to be illustrated with any ray of truth: a curse on your memory, to be always revolving in the bitterness of a late and fruitless repentance, the shortness and vanity of past pleasures: a curse upon the imagination, ever representing present and future miseries: a curse upon the will, obstinate in evil, to be torn in pieces with a thousand violent, and, withal, opposite desires, and unable to accomplish any of them: a curse, in fine, upon the whole soul, to be a hell to itself for all eternity! Good God! let it never be our misfortune to incur this dreadful curse!

5. Consider, how, after sentence is given, the elect shall enter without delay upon the possession of that everlasting kingdom which God has prepared for those that serve him, where sorrow can have no place, and joy no end. But as for the wicked, the earth shall immediately open and swallow them all down at once, with the devils who seduced them, into the bottomless pit, and the gate shall be shut, never, never more to be opened. This is the end of all worldly pride: this is the end of all carnal pleasure. Oh! how horrid a thing it is to fall into the hands of the living God! Heb. x. 31.

THE THIRTEENTH DAY.

On hell.

CONSIDER, that as it is said in holy writ, that neither eye has seen, nor ear heard, nor has it entered into the heart of man what God has prepared for those that serve him, 1 Cor. ii. 9. So we may truly say with regard to hell's torments, that no mortal tongue can express them, nor heart conceive them. Beatitude, according to divines, is a perfect and never-ending state, comprising at once all that is good, without any mixture of evil. If, then, damnation be opposite to beatitude, it must needs be an everlasting deluge of all that is evil, without the least mixture of good, without the least alloy of ease, without the least glimpse of comfort; a total privation of all happiness and a chaos of all misery.

2. Consider, more in particular, what damnation is, and how many and how great the miseries it involves. A dying life, or rather a living death; a darksome prison; a loathsome dungeon; a binding hand and foot in eternal chains, and a land of horror and misery; a lake of fire and brimstone; a bottomless pit; devouring flames; a serpent ever

gnawing; a worm that never dies; a body always burning and never consumed; a feeling always fresh for suffering; a thirst never extinguished; perpetual weeping, wailing and gnashing of teeth. No other company but devils and damned wretches, all hating and cursing one another; all hating and cursing God; spirits always in an agony, and sick to death, yet never meeting with this death, which they so much desire; cast forth from the face of God into the land of oblivion; none to comfort, none to pity them; wounded to the heart with the sense of lost happiness; and oppressed with the feeling of present misery. And all these sufferings everlasting, without the least hope of end, of intermission, or abatement. This is a short description, drawn, for the most part, from God's unerring word, of the miseries which eternal damnation imports; this is the bitter cup, of which all the sinners of the earth must drink, Ps. lxxiv.

3. Consider, that God in all his attributes is infinite: as in his power, wisdom, goodness &c: so in his avenging justice too. He is a God in hell as much as in heaven. So that by the greatness of his love, mercy and patience here, we may measure the greatness of his future wrath and vengeance against impenitent sinners. By his infinite good-

ness he has drawn them out of nothing; he has preserved and sustained them for a long time; he has even come down from his throne of glory, and suffered himself to be nailed to a disgraceful cross for their eternal salvation; he has frequently delivered them from the dangers to which they were daily exposed; patiently borne with their insolence and repeated treasons, still graciously inviting them to repentance. Ah! how justly does patience, so long abused, turn at length into fury! Mercy at last gives place to justice; and a thousand woes to those wretches that must for ever feel the dreadful weight of the avenging hand of the living God!

4. Consider, and in order to understand something better what hell is, set before your eyes a poor sick man lying on his bed, burning with a pestilential fever, attended with a universal pain over all his body, his head perfectly rent asunder, his eyes ready to fly out, his teeth raging, his sides pierced with dreadful stitches, his belly racked with violent cholic; his reins with the Stone and gravel; all his limbs tormented with rheumatic pains; and all his joints with the gout; his heart even bursting with anguish, and he crying out for a drop of water to cool his tongue. Could any

thing be conceived more miserable! and yet, let me tell you, this is but an imperfect picture of what the damned must endure for eternity; where these victims immolated to the justice of God, shall be salted all over with fire; and endure in all the senses and members of their body, and in all the faculties of their souls most exquisite torments!

5. Consider, that the state of the poor sick man, of whom we have just now been speaking, how deplorable soever it may seem, might still be capable of some alloy or ease, or some degree of comfort: a good bed to lie on; a good friend to encourage or condole with him; a good conscience to support him; a will resigned to the will of God, and, in fine, a certain knowledge that his pains must shortly abate, or put an end to his life. But the damned have nothing of all this. Their bed in hell is a lake or pit burning with fire and brimstone, to which they are fastened down with eternal chains. Their companions are merciless devils, or what will be to them worse than devils, the unhappy partners of their sins. Their conscience is ever gnawed with the worm that never dies. Their will is averse from God, and continually struggling in vain with his divine will. And what comes

in to complete their damnation, is a despair of ever meeting with an end or abatement of their torments. Good God! what would not a prudent man do to prevent the lying but for one night in torments in this life? And where then are our faith and reason, when we will do so little for escaping the dreadful night of hell's merciless flames!

THE FOURTEENTH DAY.

On the exterior pains of hell.

CONSIDER the description which Holy Job gives us of hell: Job x. when he calls it a darksome land and covered with the obscurity of death; a country of misery and darkness, where no order but everlasting horror dwells. In this gloomy region, no sun, no moon, no stars appear; no comfortable rays of light, not even the least glimpse, are ever to be seen. The very fire that burneth there, contrary to the natural property of that element, is black and darksome, and affords no light to the wretches it torments, except it be to discover to them such objects as may increase their misery. Christians, what would you think were you to be sentenced to pass the remainder of your days in some horrid dungeon, or hole, deep under ground, where you could never see the light? Would not death itself be preferable to such a punishment? And what is this to that eternal night to which the damned are sentenced? The Egyptians were in a sad condition, when for three days the whole kingdom was covered with dreadful darkness, caused by such gross exhalations, that they might even be felt by the hand. But this misery was soon over, and they were comforted by the return of light. Not so the damned in hell; whose night shall never have a morning, nor ever expect the dawning of the day!

2. Consider, that the horrors of this eternal night shall be beyond measure aggravated by the dismal music, with which those poor wretches shall be for ever entertained in this melancholy abode, — the dreadful curses and blasphemies, — the insulting voices of the tormentors, and the bowlings, the groans and shrieks of the tormented, &c. And that the other senses may also come in for their share in misery, the smell shall be for ever regaled with the loathsome exhalations of those infernal dungeons, and the intolerable stench of those half putrified carcases which are broiling there: the taste shall be oppressed with a most ravenous hunger and thirst, and the feeling, with an insupportable fire.

3. Consider, that of all bodily torments, which we can suffer in this world, there is none more terrible than to burn alive: but, alas! there is no comparison between burning here, and burning in hell. All our fires upon earth are but painted flames, if compared to the fire of hell. The fire of

this world was made to serve us, and to be our comfort: that of hell was created to be an instrument of God's vengeance upon sinners. The fire of this world cannot subsist without being nourished by some combustible matter, which it quickly despatches and consumes: the fire of hell, kindled by the breath of an angry God, requires no other fuel than sin; and feeds on this without ever decaying or consuming. Oh! dreadful stain of sin, which suffices to maintain an everlasting fire! The fire of this world can only reach the body: the fire of hell reaches the soul itself, and fills it with the most exquisite torments. Ah! sinners, which of you all can dwell with this devouring fire? Which of you all can endure this eternal burning?

4. Consider, and in order to frame some better notion of hell's torments, give ear to a most authentic vision, related by St. Teresa, chap, xxxii. of her life. "As I was one day," says the saint, "in prayer, on a sudden I found myself in hell; I know not how I was carried thither; only I understood that our Lord was pleased that I should see the place, which the devils had prepared for me there, and which I had deserved by my sins. What passed here with me lasted but a very little while; yet if I should live many years, I do not believe I

should ever be able to forget it. The entrance appeared to me to resemble that of an oven very low, very narrow, and very dark. The ground seemed like mire, exceeding filthy, stinking, insupportable, and full of a multitude of loathsome vermin. At the end of it there was a certain hollow place, as if it had been a kind of a little press in a wall, into which I found myself thrust, and close pent up. Now, though all this which I have said was far more terrible in itself, than I have described it, yet it might pass for a pleasure in comparison with that which I felt in this press. This torment was so dreadful that no words can express the least part of it. I felt my soul burning in so dismal a fire, that I am not able to describe it. I have experienced the most insupportable pains, in the judgment of physicians, which can be corporally endured in this world, as well by the shrinking up of all my sinews, as by many other torments in several kinds: but all these were nothing: in comparison with what I suffered there: joined to the horrid thought, that this was to be without end or intermission: and even this itself is still little, if compared to the agony the soul is in; it seems to her that she is choked, that she is stifled, and her anguish and torture go to a degree of excess that cannot be expressed. It is too little to say, that it seems to her that she is butchered and rent to pieces: because this would express some violence from without, which tended to her destruction; whereas, here it is she herself that is her own executioner, and tears herself in pieces. Now, as to that interior fire and unspeakable despair, which comes in to "complete so many horrid torments; I own I am not able to describe them. I saw not who it was that tormented me; but I perceived myself to burn, and at the same time, to 'be cut as it were, and slashed in pieces: in so frightful a place, there was no room for the least hopes of comfort; there was no such thing as even sitting or lying down: I was thrust into a hole in a wall; and those horrible walls close in upon the poor prisoners and press and stifle them. There is nothing but thick darkness without any mixture of light, and yet I know not how it is, though there be no light there, yet one sees there all that may be most mortifying to the sight. Although it is about six years since this happened which I here relate, I am even now in the writing of it so terrified that my blood chills in my veins. So that whatsoever evils or pains I now suffer, if I do but call to my remembrance what I then endured, all that can be suffered here appears to me just nothing.' So far the saint, whose relation deserves to be pondered at leisure: for if such and so terrible torments had been prepared for her, whose life, from her cradle, setting aside a few worldly vanities which for a short time she had followed, had been so innocent, what must sinners one day expect?

5. Consider, that there is no man on earth, that has not quite lost his senses, who would be willing, even for the empire of the world, to be broiled like.a Lawrence on a gridiron, or roasted for half an hour by a slow fire, though he was sure to come off with his life; nay, where is the man that would even venture to hold his finger in the flame of a candle for half a quarter of an hour, for any reward that this world can give? Where is then the judgment of the far greater part of Christians, who pretend to believe a hell, yet live on with so little apprehension and concern, for years together, in the guilt of mortal sin; in danger every moment of falling into this dreadful and everlasting fire, having no more than a hair's breadth, that is, the thin thread of an uncertain life, between their souls and a miserable eternity! Good God! deliver us from this unfortunate blindness; from this desperate folly and madness.

THE FIFTEENTH DAY.

On the interior pains of hell.

CONSIDER, that the fire of hell and all the rest of the exterior torments which are endured there, are terrible indeed; but no ways comparable to the interior pains of the soul: that Poena Damni, or eternal loss of God, and of all that is good: that extremity of anguish which follows from this loss; that rueful remorse of a bitter but fruitless repentance attended with everlasting despair and rage: that complication of all those racking tortures in the inward powers and faculties of the soul, are torments incomparably greater than any thing that can be suffered in the body.

2. Consider, in particular, that pain of loss, which, in the judgment of divines, is the greatest of all the torments of hell; though worldlings here have difficulties of conceiving how this can be. Alas! poor sinners, so weak is their notion of eternal goods, and so deeply are they immersed in the things of this world, amusing themselves with a variety of created objects, which divert their thoughts from God's sovereign goodness, that they cannot imagine, that the loss of God can be

so great and dismal a torment, as the saints and
servants of God, who are guided by better lights,
all agree it is. But the case will be quite altered
when they shall find themselves in hell. There
they shall be convinced, by their own woeful experience, what misery it is to have lost their God;
to have lost him totally; to have lost him irrevocably; to have lost him eternally; to have lost him
in himself; to have lost him in all his creatures; to
be eternally banished from him, who was their
only happiness, their last end and sovereign good,
the overflowing fountain of all good: and in losing him to have lost all that is good, and that for
ever. As long as sinners are in this mortal life,
they many ways partake of the goodness of God,
who makes the sun to rise upon the good and
bad, and rains upon the just and unjust. All that
is agreeable in this world, all that is delightful in
creatures, and all that is comfortable in life, is
all in some measure a participation of the divine
goodness. No wonder then, that the sinner, whilst
he so many ways partakes of the goodness of God,
should not in this life be sensible of what it is to
be totally and eternally deprived of him. But in
hell, alas! those unhappy wretches shall find, that
in losing their God, they have also lost all kind
of good or comfort, which any of his creatures

heretofore afforded; instead of which, they find all things now conspiring against them, nor any way left of diverting the dreadful thought of this loss, which is always present to their minds, and gripes them with inexpressible torment.

3. Consider, that every damned soul shall be a hell to herself, and all and every one of her powers and faculties shall have their respective hells. Her memory shall be for ever tormented, by revolving without ceasing her past folly, stupidity and madness, in forfeiting the eternal joys of heaven, that ocean of bliss, which she might have obtained at so cheap a rate, and which so many of her acquaintance are now in possession of, for an empty, trifling pleasure that lasted but for a moment, and left nothing behind it but the stain of sin, and the remorse of a guilty conscience; or for some petty interest, or punctilio of honour, by which she was then robbed of all her treasures, and all her honours; and, upon account of which, she is now so miserably poor and despicable, eternally trodden under foot by insulting devils. Oh! what will her judgment then be of this transitory world, and all its cheating vanities, when, after having been millions of ages in hell, looking back from that immense eternity, and being scarcely able to find

out in that infinite duration, this little point of her mortal life, she shall compare time and eternity, past pleasures and present pains, virtue and vice, heaven and hell!

4. Consider, that the understanding of the damned shall also have its hell, in being for ever deprived of the light of truth, always employed in false and blasphemous judgments and notions concerning God and his justice, to the great increase of its own misery; and ever dwelling upon the thoughts of present and future torments, without being able for a moment to think of any thing else: so that all and every one of the torments which the damned endure, and are to endure for eternity, are every moment before the eyes of their understanding; and thus in every moment, they bear the insupportable load of a miserable eternity.

5. Consider, that as the obstinate will of the sinner has been the most guilty, so this power of the soul shall suffer in proportion the greatest torments; always seeking what she shall never find, and ever flying from what she must for ever endure. Ah! what fruitless longings, what vain wishes shall be her constant entertainment, whilst she is doomed

for eternity, never to attain to any one the least thing which she desires! Oh! who can express that violent impetuosity, with which the will of these wretches is now carried towards God; sensible as they are of the immense happiness, which is found in the enjoyment of him? But, alas! they always find an invisible hand that drives them back, or rather they always find themselves bound fast down in eternal chains, struggling in vain with that hand which they cannot resist, and unable to make the least approach towards the object of their restless desires. Hence they break forth into a thousand blasphemies; hence the whole soul is torn in pieces with a whole army of violent, and withal opposite passions of fury, envy, hatred, despair, &c. These torments of the interior powers of the soul are attended with that never-dying worm of conscience, which shall for ever prey upon those miscreants. By this is meant an eternal remorse, a bitter but fruitless repentance, which is ever racking their despairing souls. Sweet Jesus, deliver us from such dreadful complication of evils!

THE SIXTEENTH DAY.

On a miserable eternity.

CONSIDER, that what above all things makes hell intolerable is the eternity of its torments. It is this eternity, which is an infinite aggravation of all and every one of them: it is this bitter ingredient which makes every drop of that bitter cup of the divine vengeance, of which the sinners of the earth must drink, so insupportable. Were there any hopes that the miseries of the damned would one day have an end, though it were after millions of ages, hell would be no longer hell, because it would admit of some comfort. But for all those inexpressible torments to continue for ever, as long as God shall be God, without the least hope of ever seeing an end of them: oh! this it is, that is the greatest rack of the damned. Oh! Eternity! Eternity! How little do worldlings apprehend thee now! How terrible wilt thou be to them one day, when they shall find themselves ingulfed in thy bottomless abyss, there to be for ever the butt and mark of all the arrows of God's avenging justice!

2. Consider, if one short night seems so long and tedious to a poor sick man in a burning fever; if

he tosses and turns, and no where finds rest; if he counts every hour, and with so much impatience longs for the morning, which yet will bring him but little relief or comfort: what must this dreadful night of eternity be, accompanied with all the interior and exterior torments of hell! No man in his senses would purchase a kingdom, at the rate of lying for ten years on a soft bed without coming off. Ah! what misery then must it be to be chained down to a bed of fire and brimstone, not for ten years only, nor yet for ten thousand times ten, but for as many hundred thousand millions of ages, as there are drops of water in the ocean, or atoms in the air: in a word, for an immense eternity.

3. Consider, and in order to conceive still better what this eternity is, imagine with thyself, that if any one of the damned were to shed but one single tear at the end of every thousand years, till he had shed tears enough to fill the sea; what an immense space of time would this require! The world has not yet lasted six thousand years; so that the first of all the damned would not have shed six tears. And yet, O dreadful eternity! the time will certainly come, when any one of those wretches that are now in hell, may be able with

truth to say, that at the rate of one tear for a thousand years, he might have shed tears enough to drown the whole world, and fill up the immense space between heaven and earth: and well would it be, if his torments were then to have an end. But alas! after these millions of millions of ages, he shall be as far from the end of his misery, as he was the first day he fell into hell. Compute after this, if thou pleasest, as many hundred thousand millions of years as thy thoughts can reach to; nay, suppose the whole surface of the earth to be covered with numeral figures; cast up, if thou canst, this immense sum of years, and then multiply it by itself, and multiply again a second time the product by itself; and then, at the foot of this immense account, write down: here begins eternity. O terrible eternity! Is it possible, that they who believe thee should not fear thee? Is it possible, that they who fear thee, should dare to sin?

4. Consider, that in this eternity it would be some small comfort to the damned, if their pains, like those of this life, had any intermission or abatement. But, alas! their torments are always the same; their eternal fever never abates. For as their sins are always the same, and the gate of mercy and pardon is eternally shut upon them; so the

punishment of their sins shall always continue in one and the same degree of rigour, without the least remission or diminution. The rich glutton in hell, Luke xvi. has not yet been able to obtain so much as that single drop of water, for which he so earnestly begged; nor will he ever obtain it for all eternity. Nor shall length of time inure these wretches to those evils which they suffer, so as to make them the more supportable; nor shall use and custom harden them against them; but after millions of ages their torments shall be as fresh and their feeling of them the same as on the first day. O great God! who can bear thy indignation, or support the weight of thy avenging hand? O! dreadful evil of mortal sin, which can enkindle this eternal flame.

THE SEVENTEENTH DAY.

On heaven.

CONSIDER, that if God's justice is so terrible in regard to his enemies, how much more will his mercy, his goodness, his bounty declare itself in favour of his friends! Mercy and goodness are his favourite attributes, in which he most delights: his tender mercies says the royal prophet, Ps. cxliv. are over all his works. What then must his blessed kingdom be, which in his goodness he has prepared for his beloved children, for the manifestation of his riches, his glory and magnificence for all eternity; — a kingdom, which the Son of God himself has purchased for us, at no less price than that of his own most precious blood! No wonder then that the apostle cries out: 1 Cor. ii. 9. That neither eye hath seen, nor ear heard nor hath it entered into the heart of man, what God has prepared for those that love him. No wonder that this beatitude is defined by divines, a perfect and everlasting state, replenished with all that is good, without the least mixture of evil; a general and universal good, filling brimful the vast capacity of our affections and desires, and eternally securing us from all fear or danger of want or change. O!

here it is that the servants of God, as the psalmist declares, Ps. xxxv. shall be inebriated with the
plenty of God's house, and be made to drink of
the torrent of his pleasure; even of that fountain of
life, which is with him, and flows from him, into
their happy souls for ever and ever.

2. Consider, that although this blessed kingdom
abounds with all that can be imagined good and
delightful, yet there is one sovereign good, in the
sight, love and enjoyment of which consists the
essential beatitude of the soul; and that is God
himself, whom the blessed ever see face to face;
and by the contemplation of his infinite beauty,
are set on fire with seraphic flames of love, and, by
a most pure and amiable union, are transformed
in a manner into God himself; as when brass or
iron in the furnace is perfectly penetrated by the
fire, it loseth its own nature, and becometh all
flame and fire. Happy souls! What can be wanting
to complete your joys, who are in perfect possession of your God, the overflowing source of all
good; who have, within and without you, the vast
ocean of endless felicity? O the excessive bounty
of our God, who giveth his servants, in reward
of their loyalty, so great a good, which is nothing
less than himself, the immense joy of angels! O!

shall that not suffice, my soul, to make thee happy, which makes God himself happy?

3. Consider the glory and beauty of the heavenly Jerusalem, which the holy scripture, to accommodate itself to our weakness, represents to us under the notion of such things as we most admire here below. St. John, Apoc. c. 21. describing this blessed city, tells us, that its walls are of precious stones, and its streets of pure and transparent gold; that these streets are watered with the river of water of life, resplendent as crystal, which flows from the throne of God: and that on the banks of this river on both sides grows the tree of life; that there shall be no night, nor any sun nor moon, but that the Lord God shall be its light for ever. O blessed Jerusalem! O how glorious are the things that are said of thee, O city of God! But what wonder? For if our God has given us such, and so noble a palace here below, in this place of banishment, beautified with this sun, moon and stars, furnished and adorned with this infinite variety of plants, flowers, trees, and living creatures of so many sorts, all subservient to man; if, I say, he has so richly provided for us in this vale of tears and region of the shade of death, what must our eternal habitation be in the land of the living! If here

he is so bountiful, even to his enemies in giving them so commodious, so noble a dwelling, what may not his friends and servants expect in his eternal kingdom; in which, and by which he designs to manifest to them his greatness and glory, for endless ages in an everlasting banquet, which he has there prepared for his elect! Blessed by all creatures be his goodness for ever.

4. Consider the blessed inhabitants of this heavenly kingdom, those millions of millions of angels, of whom the prophet Daniel, having seen God Almighty in a vision, tells us: Dan. vii. That thousands of thousands ministered to him, and ten thousand times a hundred thousand stood before him: that infinite multitude of saints and martyrs, and other servants of God of both sexes, gathered out of all nations, tribes and tongues; and above them all, the blessed Virgin Mother of God, queen of saints and angels: their number is innumerable. But O! who can express the happiness of enjoying this pleasant company? They are all most noble, most glorious, most wise, most holy. They are all of blood royal, all kings and queens, all children and heirs of the most high God: ever beautiful and ever young; crowned with wreaths of immortal glory, and shining much more brightly than

the sun. Their love and charity for one another is more than can be conceived: they have all but one heart, one will and one soul: so that the joy and satisfaction of every one is multiplied to as many fold, as there are blessed souls and angels in heaven, by the inexpressible delight that each one takes, in the happiness of all and every one of the rest. Christians, let us imitate their virtues here, that we may come to their happy society hereafter, and with them eternally sing to our God the immortal song of Sion.

5. Consider, that what renders all the joys of heaven, and the felicity of the blessed completely great, is the eternity of this bliss, and that infallible certainty and security which they enjoy, that their happiness is ever linked with God's eternity; that as long as God shall be God, they shall be with him in his blessed kingdom. O! my soul, how pleasant, how delightful it is to look forward into this vast eternity, and there to lose thyself in this happy prospect of endless ages! O! bless thy God, who has prepared these immortal joys for the reward of such small services, and designed them for all eternity for thee! Nor shall this immense eternity render these enjoyments anywise disagreeable or tedious by the length of the posses-

sion; but as God is an endless ocean of all good, and his divine essence an inexhaustible infinite treasure of delights, so the happiness of those that eternally enjoy him shall be always fresh, always new. Conclude then, Christian soul, to contemn and forsake all that is earthly and temporal, and from this hour, to begin thy journey towards this glorious, heavenly and eternal kingdom. There thou shalt find all that thy heart can desire, immortal honours, immense riches, pure and eternal pleasures, life, health, beauty never fading, &c. O! this alone is thy true home, the land of the living.

THE EIGHTEENTH DAY.

On the small Number of the Elect.

CONSIDER these words of Christ: many are called but few are chosen; which contain a great and dreadful truth, frequently inculcated by the mouth of truth itself, to rouse unthinking mortals from their profound lethargy, into which the enemy has lulled them. This is one of those lessons, which he has laid down for a foundation of Christian morality, in his divine sermon on the mountain, where he bids us: St. Mat. vii. 13, 14. Enter in at the narrow gate, for broad is the gate, and wide is the way, that leads to damnation, and many there are that enter by it. O! how narrow is the gate and strait the way that leads to life, and few there are that find it. Hence in the same sermon, he declares to us: not every one that says to me, Lord, Lord, shall enter into the kingdom of heaven: but he that doth the will of my Father, who is in heaven: viz. by a faithful compliance with the law of God and his gospel. Without this, he assures us, that it will avail us nothing, even to have done miracles in his name. Many shall say to me in that day: (of judgment) Lord, have we not prophesied in thy name, and cast out devils in thy name, and done many wonders in thy name? And then I will declare to them: I never knew you, depart from me, ye workers of iniquity. Good God! what will become of us, if those, that have even done miracles in thy name, shall nevertheless be excluded thy eternal kingdom?

2. Consider how many ways this frightful truth has been declared or prefigured to us in the Old Testament. Of all the inhabitants of the earth, only eight souls: viz. Noah and his family, were preserved in the ark, from the waters of the deluge: of six hundred thousand of the children of Israel, who came out of the land of Egypt under the conduct of Moses, only two persons, Joshua and Caleb, entered Canaan, the land of promise; which figure the apostle St. Paul expressly applies to us Christians. 1 Cor. x. To the same effect the prophet Isaiah, chap. xxiv. 13, 14. likens those that shall escape the divine vengeance to that small number of olives that remains on the tree after the fruit is gathered; or to the fewness of the grapes that are found on the vines after a well gleaned vintage. Ah! Christians, hear then and obey the voice of your Saviour, when he says to you: St. Luke xiii. 24. Contend, that is, strive with all your force, to enter in at the narrow gate, for many, I

say to you, shall seek to enter, and shall not be able: because the generality of Christians, though they use some endeavours to enter, yet do not strive with all their force; they are not thoroughly in earnest in their seeking, and therefore shall never find. Hear again with fear and trembling the great apostle St. Peter, when he tells you, that if the just will hardly be saved, where will the sinner appear? 1 Pet. 4. 18. O my soul, let us then take care, as the same apostle admonishes, 2 Pet. i. by good works to make our election sure: and if others will go in crowds to hell, let us resolve not to go with them for company's sake.

3. Consider, that though the scripture had said nothing of the small number of the elect, yet this truth must appear evident to us, if we compare the lives of the generality of Christians with the gospel of Christ, and his holy commandments. If thou wilt enter into life, says our Lord, Mat. xix. keep the commandments. There is no other way to life everlasting. And the first and greatest of all the commandments is this: Thou shalt love the Lord thy God with all thy heart, with all thy soul, with all thy mind, and with all thy strength. Mat. xxii. Now how few are there that keep this commandment? It is easy to say, with the generality

of Christians, that we love God with our whole heart; but what is the practice of our lives? Does not self-love, vainglory, sensuality &c. on every occasion take place of God? If so, it is in vain to say we love him above all things. And yet there is no salvation without this love. Think well on this. Besides, the apostle St. James declares: chap. iv. 4. whosoever will be a friend of this world, becomes an enemy of God. And St. John: Epist. 1, chap, ii. 15. If any one love the world, the love of the Father is not in him. And Christ himself declares, that we cannot serve two masters. Matt, vi. 24. How then can we think to reconcile the conduct of the greater part of those that call themselves Christians, (whose whole study is to please the world, and to conform themselves to its false maxims, corrupt customs, and deluded vanities) with their expectation of the kingdom of heaven, which is not to be obtained but by using violence to ourselves, by renouncing this sinful world, and by a life of self-denial and mortification?

4. Consider how great a corruption is generally found even amongst the greater part of true believing Christians; and from thence make a judgment of their future lot. How few are proof against human respects, and the pernicious fear of

what the world will say! Alas! what numbers sacrifice their eternal salvation to this cursed fear, by rather choosing to forfeit the grace of God, than the false honour and esteem of this world!

How many of those, whose birth and fortune have advanced them above the level of their fellow mortals, live continually in the state of damnation, by a cursed disposition of never putting up with an affront, and of preferring their worldly honour before their conscience! Unhappy men! who by conforming themselves now to those false maxims of deluded worldlings, will be trampled under foot by insulting devils for all eternity. How few masters of families are sincerely solicitous for those under their charge, to see that instructions be not wanting, devotions be not neglected, &c. and that nothing scandalous or sinful lurk under the favour of their negligence or connivance! And yet the apostle assures us, that if any man neglect the care of his family, he is worse than an infidel. 1 Tim. v. 8. How few parents effectually take care to bring up their children from their infancy in the fear of God, and early to inspire into them the horror of sin above all evils! Ah! what a double damnation will the greater part bring upon themselves, by sacrificing these tender souls to the devil and the world, which they might with so much ease have consecrated to heaven! In fine, not to run over all states of life in particular, is it not visible that injustice, impurity, pride, detraction, &c. everywhere reign amongst Christians; and that the number of those who live up to the gospel is indeed very small? Good God! have mercy on us, and give us grace to be of the number of the few, that so we may be of the number of the saved.

THE NINETEENTH DAY.

On mortal sin.

CONSIDER, that there is not upon earth, nor even in hell itself, a monster more hideous, more filthy and abominable than mortal sin: a monster that is the first-born of the devil; or to speak more properly, is the parent both of the devil and hell. There was not in the whole universe a creature more beautiful, more perfect, more accomplished with all kinds of gifts, both of nature and grace, than was the bright angel Lucifer and his companions: yet one mortal sin, and that only consented to in thought, changed them in an instant to ugly devils, just objects of horror and abomination to God and man. What effect, think ye, will sin have upon man, who is but dust and ashes, if it blast so foully the stars of heaven? It was this monster, sin, that cast our first parents out of paradise, and condemned both them and their posterity, to innumerable miseries, and to both a temporal and eternal death. It was sin drowned the world with the waters of the flood; and daily crowds hell with millions of poor souls, to be the fuel of endless flames. Good God! deliver us from this cursed evil.

2. Consider, that sin is the death of the soul; for as it is the soul of a man, which gives life to his body, and consequently, that body is dead, from which the soul is gone; so it is the grace of God which is the life of the soul; and that soul is dead, which by mortal sin has lost her God and his grace; if, then, a dead carcase from which the soul is gone, be so loathsome and frightful, that few could endure to pass one night in the same bed with such a bed-fellow, how is it possible, unhappy sinner, that thou canst endure to carry continually about with thee a carcass of a soul dead in mortal sin, which is far more loathsome and hideous? Ah! beg of God that he would open thy eyes, to see thy own deplorable state, to detest the hellish monster sin, which thou hast so long nourished in thy breast, and which is the true cause of all thy misery.

3. Consider what the soul loses by sin; and what she gains to recompense this loss. She loses the grace of God, the greatest of all treasures; and in losing this, she loses God himself. She loses the fatherly protection and favour of God; she loses the dignity of a child of God, and spouse of Christ; she loses her right and title to an eternal kingdom; she is stript of all the gifts of the holy

Ghost, robbed of all the merits of her whole life; becomes a child of hell, and a slave of the devil; spiritually possessed by him, and with him liable to an eternal damnation: and this is all she gains by sin; because the wages of sin is death; Rom. vi. the death of the soul here, and a second and eternal death hereafter. Ah! wretched sinners, open your eyes to see and bewail your lamentable blindness, in thus exchanging God for the devil, heaven for hell.

4. Consider, that sin is infinitely odious and detestable in the sight of God, as being infinitely opposite to his sovereign goodness. He hates it with an eternal and necessary hatred; and can no more cease to hate it, than he can cease to be God. Hence if the most just man upon earth were to be so unhappy as to fall into any one, the least mortal sin, he would in that same moment become the enemy of God; and if he were to die in that guilt, he would certainly feel the weight of God's avenging justice for all eternity. Ah! Christians, never let us be so mad as to venture to be at war with God. Alas! how many and how dreadful judgments does he daily exercise upon sin and sinners! How many, in punishment of sin, are snatched away in the flower of their age by sudden

and unprovided death! How many die in despair! How many, after having long abused God's graces, are given up to a reprobate sense, to a hardness of heart, the worst and most terrible of all his judgments! O! let us tremble at the thoughts of so great a misfortune; let us be convinced that there can be no misery so great as that which we incur by mortal sin; and that we are more our own enemies, and do ourselves more mischief, by consenting to any one mortal sin, than all the men upon earth, and all the devils in hell could do us, though they were all to conspire together to do their worst: because all that they can do, so long as we do not consent to sin, cannot hurt the soul: whereas we ourselves by consenting to any one mortal sin, bring upon our own souls a dreadful and eternal death. Good God! never suffer us to be so blind as to become thus the murderers of our own souls.

5. Consider, O my soul, and tremble at the sight of that multitude of treasons against thy God, by which thou hast so often provoked his indignation in the whole course of thy life. Alas! is it not too true, that thou no sooner didst come to the use of reason than thou didst abandon thy king and thy God, under the wings of whose father-

ly protection thou hadst happily past the days of thy innocence? Ah! how early didst thou run away from the best of fathers; and, like the prodigal child, squandering away thy substance in a strange land, hast sought in vain to satisfy thy appetite with the husks of swine. Pass over in thy remembrance, in the bitterness of thy soul, all the years of thy life; and see what treasures of iniquity in thought, word and deed, will discover themselves to thy eyes: see how long thou hast unconcernedly sported thyself on the brink of a dreadful precipice, having no more than a hair's breadth betwixt thy soul and hell. Be confounded at thy past folly; admire and adore the goodness of thy God; and now at least resolve to embrace his mercy.

THE TWENTIETH DAY.

On the relapsing sinner.

CONSIDER, that if any one mortal sin is so heinous a treason against the sovereign majesty of God, as we have seen in the foregoing chapter; if every such sin is an abomination to our Lord, and the death of the soul of that unhappy sinner who is guilty of it; what must we think of the miserable condition of relapsing sinners, that is, of such Christians as are continually falling again and again into the same mortal sins, after repeated confessions and solemn promises of amendment? Alas! what can we think, but that by this method of life they are treasuring up to themselves wrath against the day of wrath; and they will in all appearance, sooner or later, draw down a dreadful vengeance on their heads? Because by every relapse their crime is aggravated, and their latter condition becomes worse than the former.

2. Consider the ingratitude, the perfidiousness, the contempt of God, which the relapsing sinner is guilty of, as often as, after his reconciliation, he returns like a dog to the vomit. He is guilty of the highest ingratitude, in treading under foot the

grace of reconciliation, by which he had been a little before raised from the dunghill of sin, and even drawn out of the jaws of hell; and by a distinguishing mercy restored to the friendship of God, to the dignity of a child of God and heir of heaven. He is guilty of a base perfidiousness, in breaking his solemn word given to God in his confession. He is guilty of a notorious contempt of the divine majesty, in banishing God from his soul, after having invited him in, and introducing satan in his place; and this, after a full knowledge and experience of both sides. Good God! to put the whole universe in balance with thee, would be a most heinous affront; since heaven, and all the powers thereof, the earth and seas, and all things therein, are less than a grain of sand, if compared to thee: what then must we think of the unparalleled injury done thee by the relapsing sinner, when putting thee and satan in the scales, he gives the preference to the devil!

3. Consider the dreadful danger to which the relapsing sinner is daily exposed, from the sword of the divine justice which hangs over his guilty head, and is daily provoked by his ingratitude and insolence. Alas! we are all mortal: we neither know the day nor the hour that will be our last;

if we be surprised by death in the state of mortal sin, as millions have been, we are irrecoverably lost. If then it is madness at any time to risk eternity, by consenting to a mortal sin, how much more, to provoke the Almighty by frequent relapses, and by a practice of abusing his graces and mercy at every turn? Ah! what multitudes of souls have been thus betrayed into that dismal pit of never-ending woe, where the worm never dies, and the fire never is quenched! Unhappy wretches! they designed as little to damn themselves as any of us do; but God will not be laughed at.

4. Consider another evil which the sinner, who frequently falls back into the same sins, has too just reason to apprehend, is the insincerity of his past repentance. For in reality, what appearance is there, that his sorrow and resolution of amendment have been such as God requires, when after so many confessions he is still the same man? True contrition is a sovereign grief, by which the penitent detests his sin above all other evils, with a full determination and firm resolution of never returning to it any more. Now how is it likely, that the relapsing sinner detests sincerely his sin above all evils, with a firm purpose of amendment, when he is soon so easily prevailed upon by the

first temptation to return to it again?

5. Consider the remedies and means, by which we are to be preserved from this pernicious evil of relapsing into mortal sin. The first is to avoid the dangerous occasions, which have drawn or probably may draw us into the same sins: without this care to fly the occasions of sin, the strongest resolution of amendment will prove ineffectual, as we daily see by woeful experience: for he that loves the danger shall perish in it. Eccl. iii. 27. No pretext of worldly concerns must here be put in balance with eternity: we must part with hand or eye sooner than lose our souls. Another main preservative against relapse, is to labour by fervent prayer, and diligent frequenting of the sacraments, to suppress the unhappy dispositions that insensibly lead thereunto; vigorously to resist the first motions to evil; and to strive with all possible diligence to root out that wretched propensity to sin, which former sins have left in the soul. Ah! how hard it is to maintain a castle, where the enemy has already surprised the avenues, and has a strong party within, ready to open the gates to him! The third and chief remedy against relapse is, for the penitent carefully to nourish in his heart a truly penitential spirit, daily to renew his

sorrow for his sins, and to recount in the sight of God, in the bitterness of his soul, all his past iniquities; daily to admire and adore that mercy, which has borne with him so long, and to value above all treasures that grace of reconciliation, by which he has been drawn out of so much misery; daily to beg of God with all the fervour of his soul, sooner to take him out of this world, than to suffer him any more to die to him by mortal sin. Good God! grant that this may be always the disposition of our souls. Amen. Amen.

THE TWENTY-FIRST DAY.

On doing penance for our sins.

CONSIDER these words of Christ: Luke xiii. 3. 5. Except you do penance, you shall all perish. Behold here a general rule; nor does our Lord make any exception. Penance then is necessary, first, for all those whose conscience accuses them of mortal sin: alas! such as these must either do penance for their sins, or burn for them for all eternity. Poor sinners! their state is most deplorable! they are playing upon the brink of hell, and every moment one or another of them is tumbling down into that bottomless pit; and is it possible they should be so unconcerned under so great and evident a danger? Why then do they not lay hold of the grace of penance, the only plank that can save them after shipwreck; the only means left for the salvation of their souls. Secondly, penance is necessary for all those, who though their conscience accuses them not at present, yet have in their past life been guilty of such mortal offences. Ah! Christians, any one mortal sin is enough for us to do penance for all our life. And how can we do less, if we consider what mortal sin is; what it is to have been the enemies of God; what it is to have been under the sentence of eternal damnation; and never certainly to know whether this sentence has been cancelled? Is not this sufficient to oblige us to a penitential life? Can we otherwise pretend to be secure? Even those, (and God knows best how few they are) who are not conscious to themselves of having committed any such sin in their whole life, must not therefore think themselves exempt from the obligation of doing penance, as well because of their hidden sins, as those which they may have occasioned in others; for no man knows whether he be worthy of love or hatred; Eccl. ix. 1. as also because a penitential life is the best security against sin, which will insensibly prevail over us, if not curbed by self-denial, mortification and penance.

2. Consider, that as to the method of penance, different rules must be prescribed to different persons. Those who have the misfortune to be actually in the state of mortal sin, or, what is still more deplorable, are plunged into the depth of a habit of one or more kinds of mortal sin, as soon as their eyes are opened to discover the hellish monster, which they carry about with them, must, like the prodigal child, arise without delay to return to their Father. A sacrifice of a contrite and humbled

heart is what God above all things calls for at their hands; this ought to be the foundation of all their penance: without this, corporal austerities will be of small account. Such sinners ought to give themselves no rest, till they have made their peace with their God: their sins ought to be always before their eyes. Their first thoughts in the morning ought to be upon their misfortune, in being at so great a distance from their God, enslaved to the devil and liable to be his companions in eternal misery: the like ought to be their last thoughts at night; when, like the penitent David, they ought to wash their beds with their tears. As often as they appear before their God in prayer, it ought to be in the spirit of the humble publican, looking upon themselves as unworthy to lift up their eyes to heaven, or towards the altar of God; and with him, striking their breasts, with a: Lord be merciful to me a sinner. Thus will they certainly obtain mercy from him, who is the father of mercy.

3. Consider, that after the sinner has done his endeavours to seek a reconciliation with his offended God, by a sincere repentance and confession of his sins, he must not think himself exempt from any further penance, as if he had now no just debt to discharge to the justice of God, no obligation

of making satisfaction for his sins by penitential works, and of bringing forth fruits worthy of penance. This would be a great and dangerous error. Nor must he content himself with barely acquitting himself of the penance enjoined by his confessor, which, it is to be feared, seldom is sufficient to satisfy fully the justice of God. Alas! if sinners were truly sensible of the enormous injury done to God by mortal sin, as true penitents must be, they would certainly do penance in another manner than too many do; they would be more in earnest in chastising their own sinful flesh by penitential works, thus making a more proportionable satisfaction for their past treasons.

4. Consider, that the true manner of doing penance for our sins, is better learnt from the holy fathers and doctors of the church, than from the loose maxims of worldlings, or the practice of too many penitents in this degenerate age. Let us give ear then to those lights of the church, and follow their directions on this important subject. "God himself has taught us," says St. Cyprian, (L. de Lapsis) "in what manner we are to crave mercy of him; he himself says: return to me with your whole heart, in fasting, and weeping, and mourning. Joel ii. Let us then return to the Lord with our

whole heart; let us appease his wrath by fasting, weeping and mourning, as he admonishes us. Let the greatness of our grief equal the heinousness of our sins. We must pray earnestly; we must pass the day in mourning, and the night in watching and weeping, spending all our time in penitential tears. Our lodging should be on the floor strewed with ashes; our covering hair-cloth &c. After having cast off the garment of Christ, we should not now seek any worldly clothing. We must employ ourselves now in good works, by which our sins may be purged away. We must give frequent alms, by which our souls may be delivered from death." So far St. Cyprian. With whom agrees St. Pacian, in his Exhortation to Penance. If any one call you to the bath, you must renounce all such delights. If any one invite you to a banquet, you must say: such invitations are for those that have not had the misfortune to lose their God. I have sinned against the Lord, and am in danger of perishing eternally. What have I to do with feasts, who have offended my God? You must make your court to the poor; you must beg the prayers of widows; you must cast yourself at the feet of the priests; you must implore the intercession of the church: you must try all means which may prevent your perishing everlastingly." And St. Ambrose: in his second book of Penance, chap. x. "Can any one imagine that he is doing penance, whilst he is indulging his ambition in the pursuit of honours, whilst he is following wine &c. The true penitent must renounce the world, must abridge even the necessary time of sleep, must interrupt it with his sighs, and cut it short with his prayers." And St. Caesarius of Aries. Hom. viii. ** As often as we visit the sick, or those that are in prison, or reconcile together those that are at variance one with another; as often as we fast on days commanded by the church; give alms to the poor that pass by our door, &c. — by these, and such like works, our small sins are daily redeemed. But this alone is not enough for capital crimes; we must add tears and lamentations, and long fasts; and give large alms to the utmost of our power." Thus, as the same saint tells us: Hom. i. "By present mortification will be prevented the future sentence of eternal death; thus by humbling the guilty will the guilt be consumed: and by this voluntary severity, the wrath of a dreadful judge will be appeased. These short penitential labours will pay off those vast debts, which otherwise everlasting burning will never be able to discharge." Christians, let us follow in practice these excellent guides.

THE TWENTY-SECOND DAY.

Against delay of repentance.

CONSIDER, that of all the deceits of satan, by which he deludes poor sinners to their eternal ruin, there is none greater or more dangerous than the one by which he persuades them to put off their repentance and conversion from time to time, till there is no more time for them. Alas! thousands and millions of poor souls have been thus betrayed into everlasting flames, who never designed to damn themselves by dying in sin, any more than any one of us at present does. But by putting off their conversion, they have, by a just judgment of God, been surprised by death, when they least expected it; and, dying as they lived, have been justly sentenced to the second and everlasting death. Unhappy wretches! who would not believe their just Judge, who so often warns them in the gospel to watch; and declares to them that otherwise he shall come at a time when they least expect him. Ah! how dreadful and how common are these unprovided deaths!

2. Consider the great presumption of sinners, who put off their reconciliation with an offend-

ed God till another time, shutting their ears to his voice, by which he calls them at present; and refusing him entrance into their heart, where he stands and knocks. Alas! if he withdraws himself they are undone for ever: how dare they then treat him with so much contempt? Is it not infinite goodness, and inexpressible condescension in his Sovereign Majesty to call after them, when they are running from him; and so earnestly to press them, without any interest on his side, to return to him who is their only good and only happiness? What then ought they not to apprehend from his justice, if they obstinately and insolently refuse to embrace his mercy? How dare they pretend to dispose of the time to come, or promise them- selves greater graces hereafter, than those which they now abuse? Do they not know that God alone is master of time and grace, and that by his just judgment those who presume to tempt him in this manner, generally speaking, die in their sins? Ah! it is too true, that he who has promised pardon to the sinner that is sincerely converted, has promised neither time nor efficacious grace to those who defer their conversion.

3. Consider the great folly of sinners, who put off their conversion to God till another time, upon

pretence of doing it more easily hereafter: whereas, both reason and experience make it evident, that the longer they defer this work, the harder it is to bring it about. And how can it be otherwise, since by this delay, and by adding daily sin to sin, their sinful habits grow daily stronger; the devil's power over them increases; and God Almighty, who is daily more and more provoked, by degrees, is less liberal of his graces, so that they become less frequent and less pressing: till at length, by accustoming themselves to resist God's grace, they fall into the wretched state of blindness and hardness of heart, the very broad road to final impenitence!

4. Consider the unparalleled madness of those who defer their conversion upon the confidence of a death-bed repentance; designing to put a cheat upon God's justice, by indulging themselves in sin all their lifetime; and then making their peace with God, when they can sin no longer. Unhappy wretches! that will not consider that God is not to be mocked: that what a man soweth, the same shall he reap. Gal. vi. 7. 8. The general rule is, that as a man lives, so he dies: a rule so general, that in the whole scripture we have but one example of a person who died well after a wicked

life, viz. of the good thief: an example so singular in all its circumstances, as to give no kind of encouragement to such sinners, as entertain a premeditated design of giving the slip to God's justice by a death-bed conversion. Ah! how dreadfully difficult must it be for a dying sinner, in whom the habit of sin by long custom is turned into a second nature, to attain to that thorough change of heart, that sincere sorrow and detestation of sin above all things, which he never thought of in his lifetime, and which now at least is certainly necessary. Ah! how deceitful too often are those tears, which are shed by dying sinners, (as we see in the case of king Antiochus) which, being wholly influenced by the fear of death, prevail not with the just Judge. And if there is so much danger, even when tears are plentifully shed, what must there be, when, as it commonly happens, either the dulness and stupidity caused by the sickness, or the pains and agonies of the body and mind are so great, as to hinder any serious application of the thoughts to the greatest of all our concerns; for if a little headache is enough to hinder us from being able to pray with any devotion, what must the agonies of death be? No wonder then that the saints and servants of God make so little account of these death-bed performances: especially as we see by daily experience, that those who have made the greatest show of repentance, when they were in danger of death, have no sooner escaped that danger, than they are the same men they were before. O Christians, let us not then be imposed upon by the false and flattering discourses of men, who are so free in pronouncing favourably of all those, who, after a life spent in sin, make some show of repentance at their death. Let us rather tremble at the deplorable case of such souls; and remember that God's judgments are very different from those of men.

THE TWENTY-THIRD DAY.

On time and eternity.

CONSIDER how precious a thing time is, which we are apt to squander away, as if it were of no value. Time is the measure of our lives, and as much as we lose of our time so much of our life is absolutely lost. All our time is given us in order to gain eternity; and there is not one moment of our time in which we may not work for eternity; and in which we may not store up immense treasures for a happy eternity: as many therefore as we lose of these precious moments, so many are there lost eternities. This present time is the only time of working: it is the only time we can call our own; and God only knows how long it will be so. It is short, it flies away in an instant, and when once it is gone, it cannot be recalled: the very moment in which we are reading this line is just passing, never, never more to return. Every hour is post-ing away, without stopping one moment, till it be swallowed up in the immense gulf of eternity: and as many of these hours or moments as are lost, are lost for ever; the loss is irreparable. Learn hence, O my soul, to set a just value upon thy present time; learn to husband it well, by employing it in good works.

2. Consider, Christian soul, what thy thoughts will be, at the approach of death, of the value of this time, which thou makest so little of at present. What wouldst thou not then give for some of those hours, which thou losest now in vanity and sin? Ah! the dreadful anguish that will rack the soul of the dying sinner, when, seeing himself at the brink of a miserable eternity, he shall wish a thousand times, but all in vain, that he could but call back one day, or even one hour of this time past, and had but the same health and strength as he formerly had, to employ it in the love of God and sincere repentance for his sins. Ah! worldlings, why will you then be so blind as not to see, that any one of these hours which you daily squander away, is indeed more valuable than ten thousand worlds!

3. Consider what will be the sentiments of the damned in hell of the value of time, when time shall be no more: how bitterly will they regret for all eternity all those hours, days, months and years, which were allowed them by the bounty of their Creator, during the space of their mortal life; by the due employment of which, they might have

prevented that misery, to which they are now irrevocably condemned; and might have made themselves eternally and infinitely happy; but, alas! they would not work whilst the time was, whilst they had the daylight before them: the night, the dismal and eternal night is now come, in which it is too late to work; and during which they shall eternally condemn their past folly and madness, in neglecting and abusing their precious time. Ah! Christians, let us be wise at their expense. But what do you think will be the sentiments of the blessed in heaven of this precious time? Truly, if it were possible, and if their happy state could admit of such a thing as grief, there is nothing those blessed souls would regret more than the loss of any of those moments, which in their lifetime had not been well husbanded: when they shall clearly see, in the light of God, what an immense increase of glory and happiness they might have acquired, by the due employment of those precious moments.

4. Consider, that as all time is short, and passes quickly away, so all temporal enjoyments, honours, riches and pleasures of this world, are all transitory, uncertain and inconstant. Only eternity, and the goods or evils which it comprises, are

truly great, as being without end, without change, without comparison; admitting of no mixture of evil in its goods, nor any alloy of comfort in its evils. Oh! the vanity of all temporal grandeur, which must so soon be buried in the coffin. Oh! how quickly does the glory of this world pass away! A few short years are more than any one can promise himself: and after that, poor sinner, what will become of thee? Alas! the worms will prey upon thy body, and merciless devils on thy unrepenting soul. Thy worldly friends will forget thee. The very stones, on which thou hast got thy name engraved, will not long outlive thee. Oh! how true is that sentence: Vanity of vanities, and all is vanity, but to love God and serve him alone? (Thomas A. Kempis.) It is thus only we shall be wise for eternity: all other wisdom is but folly.

THE TWENTY-FOURTH DAY.

On the presence of God.

CONSIDER, that God is everywhere. If I ascend into heaven, says the Psalmist, Psal. cxxxviii. 8. thou art there: if I descend into hell, thou art there. He fills both heaven and earth; and there is no created thing whatsoever, in which he is not truly and perfectly present. In him we live, in him we move; our very being is in him. As the birds, wherever they fly, meet with the air, which encompasses them on all sides; and the fishes swimming in the ocean everywhere meet with the waters; so we, wherever we are, or wherever we go, meet with God; we have him always with us; he is more intimately present to our souls, than our souls are to our bodies. Alas! poor soul of mine, how little have we thought of this? And yet it is an article of our laith, in which we have been instructed from the very cradle. Let us seriously reflect on this truth for the future: let us strive to be always with him, who is always with us.

2. Consider, that God being everywhere sees us wherever we are; all our actions are done in his sight; our very thoughts, even the most secret

motions and dispositions of our hearts, cannot be concealed from his all-seeing eye. In vain does the sinner flatter himself in his crimes, like the libertine mentioned by the wise man: Eccl. xxiii. 28. that darkness compasses him, and the walls cover me, and no one sees me: whom do I fear? Alas! the eyes of the Lord are infinitely brighter than the rays of the sun; and no darkness, no clouds, no walls nor curtains can keep out his piercing sight, which clearly sees the very centre of the soul: and no wonder that he should clearly see what passes there, where he is always present.

3. Consider, that God, who is in all places and in all things, is everywhere whole and entire, because he is indivisible; he is everywhere in all his majesty, with all his attributes, all his perfections. We have then within us, my soul, the eternal, immense, omnipotent, self-existent, infinite Lord and Maker of all things; and we are within this infinite Being; wherever we go we have him with us. He is everywhere with his omnipotence, to which all things are subject; what then have his friends to fear? He is everywhere with his infinite justice; how then can his enemies be secure? He is everywhere infinitely good to his children; his love, his kindness to them surpasses that of the

most tender mother: he watches over them with his providence; his wisdom wonderfully disposes of all things for their greater good: what comfort then must this thought of the presence of God afford his servants and those that truly fear and love him?

4. Consider, that God, being everywhere requires of us that we should everywhere take notice of his presence. Can there be an object more worthy of our attention? And shall we then be so unfortunately blind, as to amuse ourselves about every trifle that comes in our way, and let our God, the sovereign beauty and sovereign good, pass unregarded? Ah! let us never regret our being alone, since we have always in our company that infinite Being, the sight and enjoyment of whom is the eternal felicity of angels. What if we see him not with the eyes of the body, is he the less present? And have we not within us other more noble eyes, viz. the eyes of the understanding, which, assisted by divine faith, may and ought to contemplate their God, always present in the very midst of us? Ah! the sweetest repose is to be found in him; all other recreations are vain, if compared to this.

5. Consider, that God being everywhere present

requires of us, that we should comport ourselves, both as to the interior and exterior, in such manner as becomes those who are standing in his sight. The presence of a person, for whom we have a respect, is enough to put a restraint upon us from doing any thing that is light and indecent: and shall not the infinite majesty of God, in comparison with whom the greatest monarchs of the earth are less than nothing, by his presence keep us in that exterior modesty and interior reverence, which may please his eyes? Ought we not even to annihilate ourselves in the sight of this immense divinity? But, O good God, how far are we from these dispositions, as often as we dare to sin in thy almighty presence, and fly in the face of thy sovereign majesty! Alas! my poor soul, how should we be ashamed to have our sins known to such and such persons, whose esteem we covet! We should be ready even to die with confusion to have them published to the whole world. We should be very unwilling to have even our vain and ridiculous amusements, though otherwise innocent, laid open to the eyes of our neighbours. And why will we not consider the all-seeing eye of our great God, which is always upon us, which clearly discerns all that passes in the most secret closet of our heart? Why will we not reflect, that our evil thoughts being known to God, is indeed a greater shame, a greater loss of our true honour, than if they were published by sound of trumpet over the universe.

6. Consider, that God being everywhere present everywhere requires our love: he is everywhere infinitely amiable, infinitely beautiful, infinitely good, infinitely perfect: and wherever we are, he is infinitely good to us. Why then do we not love him? He is all love: Deus charitas est, says St. John, 1 Ep. iv. God is love. We have this loving and most lovely God always with us; and always in us; why do we not run to his embraces? He is a fire that ever burns: this fire is in the very centre of our souls; how then come we to feel so little of its flames? It is because we will not stand by it. It is because we will not keep our souls at home, attentive to that great guest who resides within us, but let them continually wander abroad upon vain created amusements. Turn, O my soul, into thy rest. Psalm cxiv. 7. Turn away, my soul, from all these worldly toys which keep thee from thy God; and return to him, thy true and only happiness, and in him repose for ever.

THE TWENTY-FIFTH DAY.

On the passion of Christ: and, first on our Saviour
in the garden of Gethsemani.

CONSIDER how the Son of God, who came
down from heaven, and clothed himself with our
humanity, in order to be our priest and our victim, and to offer himself a bleeding sacrifice for
our sins to his eternal Father, was pleased to begin his passion by a bloody sweat and agony, in
the garden of Gethsemani, the night before his
death. Here having left the rest of his disciples at
some distance, and taken with him Peter, James
and John, who before had been witnesses of his
glorious transfiguration on mount Thabor, he begins to disclose to them that mortal anguish, fear
and sadness, which oppressed his heart. My soul,
saith he, is sad even unto death. Matt. xxvi. that
is, with a sadness, which even now would strike
me dead, if I did not preserve myself, in order to
suffer still more for you. Sweet Jesus, what can be
the meaning of this? Didst thou not lately cry out,
speaking of thy passion, and the desire thou hadst
of suffering for us: I have a baptism wherewith I
am to be baptized, and how am I straitened till
it be accomplished? Luke, xii. Whence then this

present sadness? Was it not thou, who hast given that strength and courage to thy martyrs, not even to shrink under the worst of torments? And wert thou thyself afraid? But, O dear Lord, I plainly understand that it was by thy own choice, that thou didst condescend so far as to let thyself be seized by this mortal anguish. It was for my instruction; and that thou mightest suffer so much the more for me. I adore thee under this weakness, (if I may be allowed to call it so) no less than on thy throne of glory: because it is here, that I better discover thy infinite love for me.

2. Consider how our dear Saviour under this sadness and anguish betakes himself to prayer, the only sure refuge under all afflictions, the only shield in the day of battle. But take notice, my soul, with what reverence he prays to his eternal Father, prostrate on the very ground: with what fervour, with a loud cry and tears, says the apostle: Heb. v. 7. and learn to imitate him. In this prayer he condescended so far as to allow the inferior part to petition, that the cup of his bitter passion might be removed from him; but then he immediately added: yet not my will, but thine be done: to teach us, under all trials and crosses, a perfect submission and resignation to the divine

will.

3. Consider how our Saviour made two interruptions in his prayer, to come and visit his disciples, but found them both times asleep. Ah! my soul, is it not thy case, like these apostles, to sleep, that is, to indulge thyself in a slothful, sensual way of living; whereas the whole life of thy Saviour was spent in labouring for thy salvation; and all that he now suffers, he suffers for thee? Ah! pity now at least his comfortless condition, whilst on the one hand his Father seems deaf to his prayers, and on the other hand his disciples are too drowsy to give any attention to him. In this desolate state, an angel from heaven appears to comfort him who is the joy of angels. Oh! what humility! But what kind of comfort, think you, did this angel bring? No other, to be sure, but the representing to him the will of his eternal Father, and humbly entreating him, in the name of heaven and earth, not to decline the imparting to poor sinners, by his infinite love, that plentiful redemption, for which he came into the world, and to undergo the ignominies and torments of one short day's continuance, with the prospect of the salvation of mankind, and of that eternal glory and honour which the Godhead would receive from all his sufferings.

Let the like consideration of God's will, his greater honour and glory, and the good of thy own soul, comfort thee also under all thy anguish and crosses. There can be no more solid comfort.

4. Consider the mortal agony which our Saviour suffered in his soul, during the prayer of this night. We may judge of the pains and anguish of his soul, by the wonderful effect they produced in his body, by casting him into that prodigious sweat of blood to such a degree, as to imbue the very ground on which he lay prostrate. Sweet Jesus, who ever heard of such an agony as this? But what thinkest thou, my soul, was the true cause of all this anguish, and of this bitter agony of thy Saviour? Chiefly these three: first, a clear view and lively representation of all that he was to suffer during the whole course of his passion: so that all the ignominies and torments, that he was afterwards successively to go through, were now all at once presented before the eyes of his soul with all their respective aggravations; by which means he suffered his whole bitter passion twice over; once by the hands of his enemies, and another time by his own most clear and lively imagination of all that he had to suffer. But why, dear Jesus, these additional agonies? Only thy love can answer

me. Another cause that contributed to our Saviour's anguish was, a distinct view of all the sins of the world from the first to the last; of all the horrid crimes and abominations of mankind, all now laid to his charge, to be cancelled by the last drop of his blood. Ah! how hideous, how detestable were all these hellish monsters in the eyes of our Saviour; who alone had a just notion of their enormity, by having always before him a clear sight of the infinite majesty offended by them! O Lord, how great a share had my sins in this tragical scene! How much, alas! did they contribute to thy pains and grief! A third cause of our "Saviour's agony was the knowledge that he had of the little use that the very Christians would make of all his sufferings; to see their blindness and hardness of heart, by which they would pervert this antidote into a mortal poison, and tread under their feet his precious blood; and the eternal loss of so many millions of souls, for which he was to die. All these sad and melancholy thoughts, attacking at once the soul of our Redeemer, cast him into that mortal agony, and forced from him those streams of blood. Christians, pity now your Saviour's anguish, and resolve never more to have any hand in afflicting his tender soul by sin.

THE TWENTY-SIXTH DAY.

On our Saviour in the court of Caiphas.

CONSIDER how our Saviour arising from his prayer, having conquered all his fears, comes to his disciples, bidding them now sleep on and take their rest; for that his hour was come, and the traitor was just at hand. But thou, dear Lord, when wilt thou rest or sleep? Not till the last sleep of death, on the hard bed of the cross. Contemplate, Christians, with the eyes of your souls, the courage and readiness to suffer for you, which your Saviour shews on this occasion, by going forth to meet the traitor and his band; see with what meekness he receives the treacherous kiss of peace. And yet to make it evident that no power upon earth could take him but with his own free will, with two words: Ego sum, I am he, he struck down the whole multitude that was come to apprehend him, making them all reel back and fall to the ground. After this he delivered himself into their hands: and they having bound him, dragged him along into the city, whilst his disciples all abandoning him, ran their way, leaving him in the hands of his enemies, who presented him first before Annas, the father-in-law of the high priest, where he was insulted by a vile servant, that gave him a blow on the face. From thence they led him to the court of Caiphas, where the chief priests and elders were assembled, longing to see this new prisoner before them, and determined to make away with him, right or wrong. Follow thou thy Saviour, my soul, every step of the way, abandoned now by all his friends: contemplate this meek lamb in the midst of all these ravenous wolves, loaded with their scoffs and insolence: but carry the eyes of thy understanding still further, view the interior of his soul, and see the joy and satisfaction that he takes in complying with his eternal Father's will, and suffering for thee: and learn from hence the like disposition in all thy sufferings.

2. Consider how our Lord was no sooner brought to the court of Caiphas, the high priest, where the great council of the Sanhedrim was assembled, but immediately after a scornful welcome they proceed to his trial, and call in the false witnesses, who were to depose against him. But see the providence of God: see the force of truth, and the wonderful innocence of this Lamb of God: notwithstanding all the malice of this impious court and their witnesses, men of neither honour nor

conscience, yet all that they could allege against him was either insignificant, or they could not agree in their story, which made their testimonies of no weight. But whilst thou adorest this providence, see and admire the meekness and patience of thy Saviour, who was silent under all the provocations given by these false witnesses; giving thereby a most convincing proof of his being something more than man, who could thus calmly hold his peace, whilst his reputation and life were both attacked by palpable calumnies. The malice of our Saviour's enemies being thus confounded, the high-priest arises and adjures him by the living God, to tell him if he was the Christ, the Son of God! In reverence to this adorable name, our Lord made a solemn confession and profession of the truth, teaching, by his example, all his followers, when called to the like trial, never to be ashamed of him or of his faith. Upon this, Caiphas rends his garment, crying out: Blasphemy! And they all pronounce him worthy of death. But thou, my soul, on the contrary, cry out with the angels and all the elect of God: Rev. v. 12. The Lamb that was slain is worthy to receive power, and divinity, and wisdom, and strength, and honour, and glory, and benediction, from all creatures for ever.

3. Consider how that unjust sentence against our Redeemer was no sooner pronounced by the great council, but immediately they all, with unheard-of barbarity, fell upon him like furies of hell rather than men, and discharged upon him all kinds of injuries, blows, affronts and blasphemy. See, my soul, how these hell-hounds spit in thy Saviour's face, and disgorge their filthy phlegm on that sacred forehead, where beauty and majesty sit: see, how they buffet, kick and strike him with merciless rage, whilst he with his hands tied behind him, is not able to ward off one blow, nor has any friend there to wipe his face, or afford him any other help. See, how they cover and muffle up his face with some filthy rag, and then in scorn (as if he were a mock prophet, and an impostor) at every blow they bid him prophesy who it was that struck him; besides many other affronts, which he endured with an invincible patience and fortitude.

4. Consider, that of all which our Saviour suffered in the court of Caiphas, nothing touched him so much to the quick, as the dangerous fall of Peter, the chief of all his apostles, who had received the most signal favours from him. Who, after having boasted that very night, that although all the rest of the disciples should abandon their Master,

lie would never forsake him; and that he would sooner die with him than deny him: yet see the weakness and inconstancy of human nature; at the voice of a silly maid, he forthwith denies his Master, repeats his denial a second and a third time: he began to curse and to swear that he knew not the man. Matt. xxvi. 74. Sweet Jesus! what is man? O Lord , look to me and support me by thy grace, or I shall deny thee. The causes of Peter's fall were, first, a secret pride and presumption upon his own strength; secondly, his neglect of the admonition of our Saviour, in sleeping when he ought to have watched and prayed; thirdly, his exposing himself to danger by running into ill company. See that the like causes have not the like effect in thee, by drawing thee also to deny, and even crucify thy Lord by sin. Learn to imitate the speedy repentance of this apostle, who im-mediately after his fall, going out, wept bitterly; a practice which, it is said, he ever after retained, as often as he heard the cock crow.

5. Consider how the high-priest and scribes, af-ter having given sentence of death against our Saviour, retired to take their rest, leaving him in hands that were not likely to suffer him to take any rest. O! what a night did our Lord pass in

the midst of that rabble, who, to satisfy their own cruelty and the malice of their masters, acted over and over again all that scene of inhumanity, which they had begun whilst their masters were there, and loaded him with all kinds of outrages and blasphemies. So that we may boldly affirm, that one half of what our Saviour suffered that night will not be known till the day of judgment. All these insolences he bears in silence, and even then whilst they are abusing him, is praying for them, and excusing them to his Father, and offering up all his sufferings in atonement for their sins. Sweet Jesus, give us grace to imitate thee.

THE TWENTY-SEVENTH DAY.

Our Saviour is brought before Pilate and Herod.

CONSIDER how early in the morning, notwithstanding their late sitting up, the high-priest, and his fellows in iniquity, convene a more numerous assembly of the Sanhedrim, and there again put the question to our Saviour, whether he was the Son of God; and receiving the same answer, confirm their former sentence. Yet as they did not think it safe for themselves, being subject to the Roman empire, to put this sentence into execution without the consent of Pontius Pilate, the Roman governor, they determined to carry him to Pilate, and by his authority to have him crucified; a kind of execution which their malice made choice of, because it was at the same time most ignominious, as being only for vile slaves and notorious criminals; and most cruel, as being a long and lingering death, under the sharpest and most sensible torments. Come now, christian soul, and contemplate thy Saviour, as he is hurried along the streets with his hands bound, from the house of the high-priest to the court of Pilate, attended by the whole council, and their wicked ministers publishing aloud as they go, that now all his impostures were laid open, his hypocrisy discovered, and himself. convicted of blasphemy.

See how the giddy mob, who a little while before reverenced him as a prophet, now all on a sudden join with his enemies, following him with opprobrious shouts, insulting him all the way that he goes, and discharging a thousand kind of injuries and affronts upon him.

2. Consider and view the Judge of the living and the dead, standing with his hands bound as a criminal before a petty governor; and behold the process. The chief priests and princes of the people having delivered him up, and Pilate demanding what particulars they had to allege against him, they made no scruple of inventing new calumnies; that he was a factious and seditious man, a traitor and a rebel to the government, who forbad tribute to be paid to Caesar, and set himself up for king of the Jews. Once more take notice of the invincible patience of thy Saviour, in hearing with silence such notorious falsities as they laid to his charge; so that the governor was astonished that a man could hold his peace under such accusations, which aimed at nothing less than procuring his condemnation to the worst of deaths.

However, as he plainly saw through all the dis-
guise of the high-priest and scribes, he interpret-
ed his silence in favour of our Saviour, only bog-
gling a little at the word king, and having received
full satisfaction upon that head, by being made to
understand that the kingdom of our Saviour was
not of this world, and therefore not dangerous to
Caesar's government, he determined to set him
at liberty. Admire the force of innocence, which
could even move a heathen, and one of the worst
of men, such as Pilate was, and assure thyself,
that generally speaking, patience and silence are
a thousand times better proofs of thy innocence,
than returning injury for injury, and making an
opprobrious and clamorous defence.

3. Consider how Pilate being convinced of our
Saviour's innocence, and desirous of setting him
at liberty, met with an obstinate resistance from
the malicious princes and deluded people; and
therefore understanding that our Saviour, as being
an inhabitant of Galilee, belonged to the juris-
diction of Herod, the Tetrarch of Galilee, he took
occasion from thence to rid himself of their importunity by sending him to Herod. Accompany
thy Lord, O my soul, in this new stage, and take
notice of of his incomparable meekness, whilst

he passes through the streets, lined on all sides with an insulting multitude, and echoing with their reproaches and clamours. Herod was most glad of his coming, in hopes to see some miracle, and therefore put a thousand questions to him; whilst the princes of the Jews, with untired malice were repeating all their false accusations against him: but our Lord was silent still, nor would he satisfy the curiosity of Herod, nor do any thing by which he might incline this prince to free him from that death, which he so ardently desired, as being by the decrees of heaven, the only means of our redemption. Blessed by all his creatures be his goodness for ever!

4. Consider how Herod, provoked by our Saviour's not consenting to gratify his inclinations of seeing a miracle, sought to revenge himself by treating him with mockery and scorn, exposing him to the scoffs of all his guards, and ordering him to be clothed in contempt with a white garment as with a fool's coat, or perhaps as a mock king; and in this dress sent him back again to Pilate, attended in the same manner as he came, with an insulting mob, headed by the scribes and pharisees. Stand amazed, my soul, to see the wisdom of the eternal Father treated thus as a fool;

and learn from hence not to repine, nor be solicitous about the judgment of the world.

5. Consider how Pilate, seeing our Saviour brought back again to his tribunal, contrived another way to bring him off, so as to give at the same time as little offence as might be to the high-priest and the chief of the Jews. It was the custom of that nation on the day of their paschal solemnity, (which was celebrated that very day) in memory of their delivery from the Egyptian bondage, to have one criminal set at liberty, whom the people should petition for: wherefore Pilate, taking advantage of this opportunity, proposed to their choice our Saviour, on the one hand, and Barabbas, a notorious malefactor, robber and murderer, on the other; making sure that they would rather choose to have the innocent Lamb of God released, than Barabbas, the worst of criminals, to escape due punishment. Ah! Pilate, what an outrageous affront dost thou here put upon the Son of God, whilst thou pretendest to favour him! What! must the Lord of life and immortality, the King of heaven, stand in competition with the vilest of men, with the most notorious criminal that could be pitched upon? Must it be put to the votes of the mob, which of the two is the better man,

and which the more worthy of death? O the unparalleled injury! o! the unparalleled humility of
my Saviour! o! King of glory, how low hast thou
stooped to raise me up from the dunghill!

6. Consider, if it was an intolerable affront to
compare our Saviour with Barabbas, what idea
must we frame, or what name must we give to
that blind people's choice, when they preferred
Barabbas to Christ, and desired that the latter
might be crucified, and the former acquitted ? O !
see, my soul, in this wonderful humiliation of thy
Lord, how deep, how dangerous was the wound of
pride, which could not be cured but by such and
so great humility : O! see if thine be yet cured.
Examine also thyself, if thou hast not often been
guilty, like these blind Jews, of preferring Barabbas to thy Saviour ; by turning thy back to him for
some petty interest, or filthy plea sure ? If so, thou
art more inexcusable than they, because thou
knowest him to be the Lord of glory, at the same
time as thou persecutest him by sin : whereas if
they had known him to be so, they would never
have preferred a Barabbas before him.

THE TWENTY-EIGHTH DAY.

Our Saviour is scouraged at the Pillar and crowned with Thorns.

Consider, how the Jews still continuing to cry out against our Lord, and in a tumultuous manner to demand his crucifixion, Pilate contrives another way to bring about his being set at liberty, viz. by striving to satisfy their cruelty, in ordering him to he most severely scourged. O! Pilate, how cruel is thy mercy! Is it thus that thou treatest him whom, thou declarest innocent? Is this thy justice? But our sins, O my soul, required that the Lord of glory should be thus cruelly treated, and subjected to this ignominious punishment, to which none but common slaves or the meanest wretches are liable, and to which a Roman citizen could upon no account be condemned. Stand thou, my soul, and see in what manner this sentence is executed. Behold how the bloody soldiers lay their impious hands on this meek Lamb of God, how they strip off all his clothes, and tie him fast to a stony pillar; see how they discharge upon his sacred back and shoulders innumerable stripes, lashes and scourges: behold the blood come spouting forth on all sides; see how his body is all rent and mangled by their cruelty, and the flesh laid open to the very bones; behold bis enemies all the while insulting over him, and rejoicing at his torments; whilst he, with eyes cast up towards heaven, is offering up all that he suffers for their sins, and for those of the whole world. Ah sinners, take a serious view of your Redeemer's condition, and contemplating in his torn and mangled body, the malice of sin, learn to detest this hellish monster, which has brought on the Son of God all these sufferings.

2. Consider, how these bloody ruffians by their cruel scourging having made but one wound of our Saviour's body, from head to foot, loose him at last from the pillar, leaving him to put on his clothes as well as he could. Ah! Christians, have compassion now on your Saviour's abandoned condition; who has no one to lend him an helping hand to bind up his gaping wounds, or stanch the blood that comes flowing from them! O! present yourselves now, and offer him what service you are able: offer at least to assist him in putting on his clothes, to cover his green wounds from the cold air. But, O how rough are these woolen cloaths to his wounded hack! Alas! instead of affording him any fuse or comfort, they do but increase His sores, by their rubbing upon them.

3. Consider how the bloody soldiers had scarce given our Saviour a short respite after his scourging, when they were pushed on by the devil to act another scene of cruelty, such as never was heard of before or since: and that was to make themselves a barbarous sport, in crowning him for a king. Therefore they drag him into the court of the Proetorium, and assemble together the whole regiment: then violently strip him again of all his clothes, which now begin to cleave to his wounded body; set him on a bench or stool, throw about him some old ragged purple garment, twist a wreath of long hard and sharp thorns, and press it down on his sacred head, put in his hand for a sceptre a reed or cane: then in derision, coming one by one, they bend their knees before him, with a scornful salutation, Hail, King of the Jews; they spit in his face, buffet him, and taking the reed or cane out of his hand, strike him with it on the head, so driving the thorns deeper in, whilst the blood trickles down apace from the many wounds which he receives from their points. Sweet Jesus, what shall we here say, or which shall we most admire, the malice of these ministers of Satan, or thy unparalleled charity, which made thee undergo such unheard of reproaches and torments for ungrateful sinners? Blessed be thy

goodness for ever.

4. Consider how Pilate, hoping now that the rage and malice of the Jews would be satisfied, so as to insist no longer upon our Saviour's death, after they should see with how much cruelty and contempt he had been treated in compliance with their fury, leads him forth as he was with his crown of thorns on his head, and his ragged purple on his shoulders; and from an eminence shews him to the people, with an Ecce homo, Behold the man. Behold in what manner he has now been handled; cease then to seek his death any longer. Let his body, mangled from head to foot, bespeak your pity. But thou, Christian soul, behold the man, with other kind of eyes than these hard-hearted wretches: and see to what a condition thy sins and his own infinite charity have reduced him. Behold his head crowned with a wreath of sharp thorns, piercing on all sides his sacred flesh, and entering into his temples with excessive pain. Behold his face quite disfigured with blows and bruises, and all besmeared with spittle and blood. Behold his whole body inhumanly rent and torn with whips and scourges; and now covered with a hard ragged garment, rubbing and at each moment increasing his wounds:

and then look up and contemplate him upon his throne of glory, and see what return thou canst make him for having thus annihilated himself for the love of thee. He desires no more of thee than an imitation of his patience and humility: see, then, in what manner thou art to practise these lessons.

THE TWENTY-NINTH DAY.

Our Saviour carries his Cross, and is nailed to it.

CONSIDER how the malice of the Jews, no ways relenting at the sight of the Lamb of God bleeding for the sins of the world, but continuing still in a tumultuous manner to demand that he might be crucified, Pilate at last yields to their importunity, and against his own conscience, sentences our Saviour to the death of the cross. Ah I Christians, has it never been your misfortune, by the like cowardice, to condemn your Saviour and his doctrine, and basely to renounce in the practice of your lives the maxims of his gospel, for fear of what the world would say? Has not too often a much weaker temptation than the fear of losing Caesar's friendship, induced you to crucify again the Son of God? Be confounded and repent.

2. Consider how this sentence of death, how unjust soever from Pilate, yet as being most just from his eternal Father, and necessary for our salvation, was received with perfect submission, charity and silence by our Redeemer; who thereupon was immediately stripped again of his purple garment, and clad with his own clothes; and a

heavy cross, of length and bigness proportionable to the bearing of a man, was laid on his wounded shoulders; and two thieves or highway robbers were appointed to bear him company, and to be executed with him; to verify that prophecy: With the wicked he was reputed. Isai. liii. Come now, devout souls, and take a view of our Lord in this his last progress or procession. A crier leads the way, publishing aloud the pretended crimes and blasphemies of this never heard of malefactor: then follow the soldiers and executioners with ropes, hammers, nails, &c. After these goeth, or rather creepeth along", our high-priest and victim, all bruised and bloody, with a thief on each hand, and the cross on his shoulders, dragging it forward step by step, followed and surrounded on all sides by the priests, the scribes, and the whole mob of the people, cursing, reviling and scoffing at him: whilst the cruel hangmen are hastening him forward with their kicks and blows. Ah! Christians, now at least take pity on your Saviour's sufferings, and add not to his load by sin.

3. Consider how our blessed Lord, having for some time, with unspeakable labour and torment, carried his cross through the streets, at last falleth down under the weight, unable to carry it any fur-

ther. Wonder not, my soul, at this; since, besides the load of the cross oppressing his wearied body, wounded on every part, and exhausted by the loss of so much blood, his heavenly Father has laid upon his shoulders another more insupportable weight, viz. that of the sins of the whole world. Ah! Christians, it is under this intolerable burthen that your Saviour faints and falls down. Nor is he any way eased of this merciless load by Symon of Cyrene, who was compelled to take up the cross, but bore no part of the weight of our iniquities; all which the heavenly Father laid upon his beloved Son, to be cancelled with his blood and death. O infinite goodness of the Father! O infinite charity of the Son! to do and suffer so much for wretched man. O my soul, see thou never more be ungrateful to so loving a God.

4. Consider how our Saviour being now arrived at Mount Calvary, quite wearied and spent, the ministers of hell still persecute him with unwearied cruelty; and whereas it was the custom to give to the criminals that were to die a strengthening draught of wine seasoned with myrrh, they contrived to mingle gall with the potion designed for him. After this they violently stripped him of his clothes, now cleaving fast to his sores, and thus

opened again his wounds, and exposed him naked to shame and cold in the sight of an immense multitude. Draw nigh now, my soul, and see him bleeding afresh for the love of thee. Oh! see how, while the cross is preparing, he falls upon his knees, and offers himself to his eternal Father a bleeding victim to appease his wrath enkindled by thy sins.

5. Consider how the cross lying flat on the ground, they lay our dear Redeemer stretched out upon it, who like a meek lamb makes no resistance. And first drawing his right hand to the place designed to fix it on, they drive with their hammers a sharp gross nail through the palm of his hand, forcing its way with incredible torment through the sinews, veins, muscles and bones, of which the hand is composed, into the hard wood of the cross: in the meantime the whole body, to favour that wound and the pierced sinews, was naturally drawn towards the right side, but not long permitted to remain so; for immediately these cruel butchers laying hold of his other arm and hand, violently drag him towards the left side, in order to nail that hand also to the place designed for it. Then pulling down his legs, they fastened bis sacred feet in like manner with nails

to the wood: and all this with such violent cruelty, that, it is thought, with stretching and pulling
they very much strained his whole body, and disjointed it in many parts, according to that of the
royal prophet: They have dug my hands and feet;
they have numbered all my bones. Ps. xxi. Ah!
Christians, if the contracting or piercing of any
one nerve or sinew, if the disjointing or displacing
of any one bone, ever so small, is so cruel a torture, what must we think of the torments which
our Saviour endured in his disjointed body? What
must we think of what he suffered, when his
hands and feet, where so many sinews, muscles,
veins and bones all meet, were violently bored
through with gross nails! Oh! let us never cease to
admire, adore, and love his mercy.

THE THIRTIETH DAY.

Our Saviour on the cross.

CONSIDER how the bloody executioners, having now nailed our Saviour fast to the cross, begin with ropes to raise him up in the air. O! what shouts did his enemies now make, when he appeared above the people's heads. With what blasphemies did they salute him, whilst his most afflicted mother, and other devout friends are pierced to the heart at the sight! At length they let the foot of the cross fall into the hole prepared for it, with a jolt, by which our Saviour's mangled body was not a little injured, and the wounds of his hands and feet widened, and thus he now hangs, poised in the air, in most dreadful pangs and torments, the whole weight of his body sustained by his pierced hands and feet, by which his wounds are continually increased; no place to rest his head on. but upon thorns; no other bed for his wearied and wounded body, but the hard wood of the cross.

2. Consider the infinite charity of our Saviour, and the unparalleled malice of his enemies. He, amidst his torments, cries out: Father, forgive

them, for they know not what they are doing. They grin and shake their heads at him, saying: Vah! thou that destroyest the temple of God and in three days dost rebuild it, save now thy own self: if thou art the Son of God, come down from the cross: with a thousand other reproaches and blasphemies, with which he is loaded, not only by the common people and soldiers, but also by the chief priests, scribes and elders, which he hears and bears in patience and silence. But, O! who can tell us the interior employment of his blessed soul all this while that he hangs upon the cross, — his thoughts of peace towards us, his prayers for us, the anguish and dreadful agonies of the interior part of his soul, and the inexpressible joy in the supreme part thereof, in the glory of his Father, which was to arise from that plentiful redemption, which he was then imparting to poor sinners!

3. Consider the part that the blessed Virgin Mother bore in the sufferings of her son: and how truly here was verified that prophecy of old Simeon: Thy own soul a sword shall pierce, O! how killing a grief must have oppressed this most tender and most loving of all mothers, when, during the whole course of the passion of her dearest Son,

whom she loved with an incomparable love, she was an eye-witness to all the injuries, outrages and torments that he endured. Ah! blessed Lady, may we not truly say that the whips, thorns and nails, that pierced thy Son's flesh, made as deep a wound in thy virgin heart: and that nothing but a miracle could have supported thy life under such excess of pain? But, O! what a deep wound didst thou feel in thy soul, when thy dying Son recommended thee to his beloved disciple, St. John, giving to thee the son of Zebedee in exchange for the son of God! Blessed Virgin, we gladly acknowledge thee for our mother, bequeathed to us all in the person of St John. Oh! by all thy sufferings, remember us poor banished children of Eve, before the throne of grace. Christians, learn the admirable lessons which our Lady teaches you at the foot of the cross; learn her unshaken faith and undoubted hope; learn her perfect resignation, patience and fortitude. Oh! learn from her to love Jesus, and detest sin, the true cause of his sufferings.

4. Consider how all things seem now to have conspired against our dearest Lord. His father has forsaken him; his mother's presence and grief pierce him to the heart. As for his own apostles,

one of them has betrayed him; another has denied Him; all have abandoned him; his friends, and those whom he had most favoured and miraculously cured, now either join with his persecutors, or at least are ashamed of him: his enemies triumph and insult over him; his own body by its weight is a torment to him. But what most of all afflicts him, is to see the ingratitude of Christians, the little benefit they will make of his death and passion, and the eternal loss of so many souls redeemed by his precious blood. Ah! sweet Jesus, suffer me not to be one of that unhappy number: suffer me not to be so miserable, as to join with thy enemies in crucifying thee by sin!

5. Consider the lessons that our Saviour gives us by his last words upon the cross: 1st. Of perfect love and charity to his enemies, by praying for them, and excusing them to his eternal Father: Father, forgive them, for they know not what they do. Oh! let us learn from our dying Redeemer this necessary lesson, to love and pray for those that hate and persecute us: and instead of aggravating their crime, to excuse it and impute it to their ignorance. Oh! how true is it of every sinner, he knows not what he is doing, otherwise he would never dare to fly in the face of infinite majesty: he

would never be so mad as to renounce heaven for a trifle, and cast himself down the precipice that leads to hell. 2dly, learn the efficacy of a sincere conversion, and an humble confession of sins, in the plenary indulgence given by our dying Saviour to the good thief: Amen, I say unto thee, this day thou shalt be with me in paradise. 3dly, learn a filial devotion to the Virgin Mother, recommended to us all by her Son, in the person of St. John: Behold thy mother. 4thly, learn the greatness of the interior anguish of thy Saviour's soul, from these words: My God! my God! why hast thou forsaken me? Alas! it was for no other reason, but that poor sinful man might not be forsaken. 5thly, from that word of thy crucified Jesus, I thirst: take notice of two violent thirsts which thy Saviour endured upon the cross; the one corporal, proceeding from his having fasted so long, passed through so many torments, and shed so much blood: the other spiritual, in his soul, by the vehement desire of our good and salvation. But, Oh! cruel wretches, who would give him nothing but vinegar to quench his corporal thirst! More cruel sinners, who instead of satisfying his spiritual thirst by gratitude and devotion, give him nothing but the gall and vinegar of sin and wickedness! 6thly, from these words of our dying Saviour, It is consummated, learn to rejoice that the whole work of man's redemption is now perfected; that the figures and prophecies of the law are fulfilled; and the handwriting that stood against us is now completely cancelled by the blood of our Redeemer. 7thly, from these last words of our expiring Lord: Father, into thy hands I commend my spirit, learn both in life and death to commit thyself wholly to thy God. Happy they that study well these lessons which their great Master teaches them from the chair of his cross.

THE THIRTY-FIRST DAY.

On the Death of our Saviour.

CONSIDER how our Lord having spoken these last words: Father, into thy hands I commend my spirit, with a loud and strong voice, bowing down his head in perfect submission to his Father's will, and perfect charity to us poor sinners, to whom in this posture, he offered as it were the kiss of peace, breathed forth his pure soul, and thus ended his mortal life; which from the moment of his birth till now, had been nothing else but a series of sufferings endured for us. Hasten now, my soul, and approach boldly to kiss the sacred feet of thy Redeemer, view his pale limbs, count at leisure all his wounds, and lament all thy sins, for which he suffered such exquisite torments.

2. Consider in the passion of our Saviour the truth of these words, which were delivered by him on another occasion, He that humbleth himself shall be exalted: and see how our Lord, having humbled himself to the death of the cross, was even at the very time honoured and exalted by his heavenly Father, and that many ways; for during the time he hung upon the cross, the sun for three

whole hours withdrew his light; and at his death, the earth trembled, the rocks were split, and the monuments opened; the veil of the temple, which hung before the sanctuary, was rent from top to bottom; the people, touched by these wonders, went home striking their breasts; and the centurion, or captain of the guards, publicly professed, that this man whom they had crucified, was truly the Son of God. Rejoice, O Christian soul, to see thy Saviour's death thus honoured; and learn under all events to confide in God, who will at last convert the malice of thy enemies to thy honour and advantage. Sit now down at the foot of the cross, and there at leisure meditate.

3. Consider, and repeat in thy mind, the multitude and variety of the sufferings, which thy Saviour has endured for thee, from his entrance into the garden of Gethsemani, till his expiring on the cross. View them one by one, and thou shalt see that not one part of his sacred body (which being the most perfect, was at the same time the most sensible of pain of any that have ever been), was free from its peculiar torment: his head crowned with thorns; his face defiled with spittle, bruised, and swollen black and blue with blows; his hair and beard plucked and torn; his mouth drenched

with gall and vinegar; his shoulders oppressed
with the weight of the cross; his hands and feet
pierced with nails; his whole body exhausted
with a bloody sweat; mangled and laid open with
whips and scourges; his limbs wearied out, and
all disjointed upon the cross. What he suffered in
his soul was not one jot less, but rather infinitely
more than what he suffered in his body. Witness
that mortal anguish which cast him into his agony
in the garden; witness that grievous complaint on
the cross: My God! my God! why hast thou forsaken me? He suffered moreover in his reputation
(which is often dearer to a man than life). by false
witnesses, and outrageous calumnies and depo-
sitions. He suffered in his honour by all kinds of
reproaches and affronts; he suffered in his goods,
being despoiled of his very clothes, and hanging
naked upon the cross; he suffered in his friends,
being forsaken by them all: not to speak of other
sufferings, which are usually most sensible to flesh
and blood: viz. the ingratitude of those whom
he had favoured with his miracles, the triumphs
of his enemies, their insults over all his disciples, &c.: — and in all these sufferings, he denied
himself those comforts which he usually affords
his servants under their crosses, and which have
made the greatest torments of the martyrs not

only tolerable, but oftentimes sweet and comfortable. But he would allow himself no other comfort, than that of doing the will of his Father, and purchasing our redemption.

4. Consider who it is that suffers all this; and thou shalt find, that he is the eternal Son of God, equal and consubstantial to the Father: the great Lord and Maker of heaven and earth, infinite in power, infinite in wisdom, infinite in all perfections. But for whom does he suffer all this? For poor man, a wretched worm of the earth; for ungrateful sinners, traitors to his eternal Father, and to himself; for those very Jews that crucified him; for us mortals, who for the most part were likely never to thank him, or even so much as to think of his sufferings. O, how admirable, art thou, O Lord, in all thy ways, but in none more than in the contrivances of thy mercy! O, how does this passion of our Redeemer set out and illustrate all the attributes of God! It is here we discover his infinite goodness and charity, in thus wonderfully communicating himself to us. It is here we discover his unparalleled mercy, in taking upon himself our miseries, and enduring the stripes due to our sins. Here we see the admirable wisdom of his providence, in opening to us by his own death the

fo mi tain of life. Here we learn to fear his justice, which fell so heavily upon his own Son, who had but clothed himself in the resemblance of a sinner, in order to make atonement for our sins. Oh! what must the guilty themselves one day expect at his hands, if they do not prevent the terrors of his justice, by laying hold of his present mercy!

5. Consider, in the sufferings of thy Saviour, the infinite malice, the unparalleled heinousness of mortal sin, which was not to be cancelled, but by the last drop of blood of the Son of God. This is one of the chief lessons which thy Saviour desires to teach thee from the cross; thou canst not please him better than by studying well this lesson. Oh! never be so ungrateful as to crucify him again by mortal sin. Oh! let not that monster live in thee, for the destroying of which Christ himself would die.

RULES

for a

CHRISTIAN LIFE.

To be observed by all that desire to secure to themselves a happy eternity.

Settle in thyself a firm resolution, on no account whatever, to consent to mortal sin. This resolution is the very foundation of a virtuous life: whosoever is not arrived thus far, has not yet begun to serve God. Without this resolution, it is in vain for any one to flatter himself with the hopes of living holily or dying happily.

2. In order to enable thyself to keep this resolution, be diligent in flying all dangerous occasions, such as bad company, lewd or profane books, immodest plays, &c. "For he that loves the danger, shall perish in it." Eccl. 3. v. 27.

3. Watch all the motions of thy heart, and resist the first impressions of evil; keep a guard on thy senses and thy imagination, that the enemy may not surprise thy soul through these avenues. Con-

temn not small faults, lest by degrees, you fall into greater.

4. Fly an idle life, as the source of all mischief; and take it for a certain truth, that an idle life will never bring a Christian to heaven.

5. Never omit, upon any account, thy morning and evening prayers. In the morning, remember always to present to God the first fruits of the day, by giving him thy first thoughts. Make him an offering of all the actions of the day, and renew this oblation at the beginning of every thing thou dost. "Whether you eat or drink," says St. Paul, (1 Cor. x. v. 3.) " or whatsoever else you do, do all for the glory of God.

6. At thy evening prayers, make a daily examination of thy conscience, calling thyself to an account how thou hast past the day; and whatever sins thou discoverest, labour to wash away by penitential tears, before lying down to sleep. Who knows but that night will be thy last? In going to bed, think on the grave; compose thyself to sleep in peace with thy God: and if thou awakest in the night, raise thy thoughts to him who is always watching over thee.

7. Besides morning and evening devotions, set aside some time in the day for prayer, more particularly mental, by an interior conversation of thy soul with God, her only true and sovereign good. In the midst of all thy employments, keep thyself as much as possible in the presence of God, and frequently aspire to him by short ejaculations. Read spiritual books often, as letters or messages sent to thee from heaven; and if thy circumstances permit, assist daily at the sacrifice of the Mass.

8. Frequent the Sacraments, at least once a month, and take especial care to prepare thyself to receive them worthily.

9. Have a great devotion to the Passion of Christ, and often meditate on his sufferings.

10. Be particularly devout to his blessed mother; take her for thy mother, and seek upon all occasions, her protection and prayers; but learn withal to imitate her virtues.

11. Let not a day pass without offering to God some acts of contrition for thy past sins; and strive to maintain in thy soul a penitential spirit.

12. Study to find out thy predominant passion, and labour with all thy power to root it up.

13. Beware of self-love as thy greatest enemy; and often use violence to thyself by self-denials and mortification; remember the kingdom of heaven is not to be taken but by violence. St. Matt. xi. 12.

14. Give alms according to thy ability: For judgment without mercy to him that has not done mercy. James ii. 13. Set a great value upon spiritual almsdeeds, by striving all thou canst to reclaim unhappy sinners; and for that end daily bewail their misery in the sight of God.

15. Be exact in all the duties of thy calling, as being to give an account one day to that great Master, who has allotted to each one of us our respective station in his family.

16. Remember always thy last end, and thou shalt never sin. Eccl. vii. 40.

THE LIFE OF FAITH.

Be ye Followers of me, as I also am of Christ,

1 Cor. xi. 1.

MEDITATE ofien of these. words of the apostle; The just man liveth by faith, Rom, i. 17. O what great things are contained in this life of faith!

The life of faith supposes, that one first dies to oneself. The spiritual death is here the beginning of life. You are dead, said the apostle, 3. and your life is hid with Christ in God.

To live in faith is to be only taken up with the objects of faith; to think only on the promises of faith; and to make our judgment of all things here below, only with respect to their agreeableness with the things of faith.

To live by faith, is to lead as to the exterior, a common life; but as to the interior, to unite oneself continually to God through Jesus Christ.

The life of faith maintains itself principally by mental prayer and the holy communion. Prayer puts to death the old man; and the holy communion gives life to the new man.

Nothing is more contrary to the life of faith, than the frequenting the high-life world, with its companies and assemblies; idle visits, vain compliments, frivolous letters, &c. But on the other hand, the life of faith grows in us by godly conversation, by an union with those who are truly good, and by the reading of such spiritual books, as are solidly pious and affecting.

The life of faith is much hindered by the tumult of business, by the trouble of scruples, by the prejudices of the mind, by the desires of seeing, of acquiring, of possessing, of pleasing, or of being esteemed; all these things destroy that life of faith, which is the life of the soul. ; The man of faith is mild, he is kind, he is courteous, he is true, he is plain and sincere, he is generous, of good counsel, of good company; he is always even in his temper, easy in his conversation, and sets no bounds to the help he is ready to afford every one under the variety of human events.

To live well the life of faith, three things are necessary. 1. To love entirely Jesus Christ. 2. To have a great contempt of the world, and of all that the world esteems. 3. To live only, and to count only for the present day.

That the life of faith may be more conformable to the life of Christ, it ought to be accompanied with these three things: the love of humiliations ; rejoicing in sufferings; and embracing poverty. All the saints have lived by faith. Amongst these heroes of faith I shall name in particular, St. Paul, St. Francis and St. Teresa.

We need but to cast one glance of the eye on what passes in the world, to see that scarce any one there lives by faith. Many people pray, frequent the sacraments, give alms, practise austerities; and yet with all this, they cease not to live in themselves, with themselves, and for themselves. They have their humours, their pretensions, their eagernesses, their vanities, their oddities, their singularities; they are unwilling to suffer, or to be forgot, or to want any thing, or to deny themselves the liberty of judging of their neighbours. They are devotees quite living of self-love: they have never known the life of God, the life of faith, the internal man, the interior union with Jesus Christ.

He who said, I live, now not I; but Christ liveth in me, Gal. ii. 20. was indeed a man of faith, a soul quite animated by faith, a heart from which the world was totally banished. He had no longer a being of his own, a life of his own; Jesus Christ was all in him, and he was all in Jesus Christ. St. Paul was this man. O let us live by faith, and we shall be cheerful, easy and happy; the kingdom of God will be in us; we shall neither fear men, nor devils, nor death. We shall have for our wealth the cross of Jesus Christ, the sacraments of Jesus Christ, the body of Jesus Christ, and our riches shall surpass the riches of kings.

THE END

www.ingramcontent.com/pod-product-compliance
Lightning Source LLC
Chambersburg PA
CBHW020539160726
47991CB00002B/500